D0782375

Selected Works of Juan Donoso Cortés

Recent Titles in
Global Perspectives in History and Politics

Power and Policy in Transition: Essays Presented on the Tenth Anniversary of the National Committee on American Foreign Policy in Honor of Its Founder, Hans J. Morgenthau
Vojtech Mastny, editor

Perforated Sovereignties and International Relations: Trans-Sovereign Contacts of Subnational Governments
Ivo D. Duchacek, Daniel Latouche, and Garth Stevenson, editors

The Pure Concept of Diplomacy
José Calvet de Magalhães

Carl Schmitt: Politics and Theory
Paul Edward Gottfried

Reluctant Ally: United States Policy Toward the Jews from Wilson to Roosevelt
Frank W. Brecher

East Central Europe after the Warsaw Pact: Security Dilemmas in the 1990s
Andrew A. Michta

The French Revolution and the Meaning of Citizenship
Renée Waldinger, Philip Dawson, and Isser Woloch, editors

Social Justice in the Ancient World
K. D. Irani and Morris Silver, editors

The European Union, the United Nations, and the Revival of Confederal Governance
Frederick K. Lister

The Leviathan in the State Theory of Thomas Hobbes: Meaning and Failure of a Symbol
Carl Schmitt
Translated by George Schwab and Erna Hilfstein

Roman Catholicism and Political Form
Carl Schmitt
Translated and annotated by G. L. Ulmen

The Early Security Confederations: From the Ancient Greeks to the United Colonies of New England
Frederick K. Lister

Selected Works of Juan Donoso Cortés

Juan Donoso Cortés

Translated, edited, and
introduced by Jeffrey P. Johnson

Contributions in Political Science, Number 389
Global Perspectives in History and Politics
George Schwab, *Series Editor*

GREENWOOD PRESS
Westport, Connecticut • London

Library of Congress Cataloging-in-Publication Data

Donoso Cortés, Juan, marqués de Valdegamas, 1809–1853.
[Selections. English 2000]
Selected works of Juan Donoso Cortés / Juan Donoso Cortés ; translated, edited, and introduced by Jeffrey P. Johnson.
p. cm.—(Contributions in political science, ISSN 0147–1066 ; no. 389)
Includes bibliographical references and index.
ISBN 0–313–31397–0 (alk. paper)
1. Conservatism. 2. Donoso Cortâs, Juan, marquâs de Valdegamas, 1809–1853—Contributions in political science. I. Johnson, Jeffrey P. II. Title. III. Series.
JC573.D6613 2000
320.52—dc21 99–056465

British Library Cataloguing in Publication Data is available.

Library of Congress Catalog Card Number: 99–056465
ISBN: 0–313–31397–0
ISSN: 0147–1066

First published in 2000

Greenwood Press, 88 Post Road West, Westport, CT 06881
An imprint of Greenwood Publishing Group, Inc.
www.greenwood.com

Printed in the United States of America

The paper used in this book complies with the Permanent Paper Standard issued by the National Information Standards Organization (Z39.48–1984).

10 9 8 7 6 5 4 3 2 1

Copyright Acknowledgments

Contents

Acknowledgments

I would like to thank Joseph Crawford and James Reinhart for proofreading the manuscript and to Luis Ortiz for checking the accuracy of my translations as well as for his invaluable technical expertise. And a special note of appreciation goes to Nicole Cournoyer for her fine work of editing. I am also grateful to Frederick Lawrence, Francis (Pat) Kilcoyne, Paul Breines, James Bernauer, S.J., and George Schwab for their invaluable advice on this project. Finally I must thank my friends Michael and Ellen Miller for the use of their peaceful and quiet home in the country, which allowed me the opportunity to work on these translations without interruptions and distractions.

Translator's Note

The works I have translated and included in this volume are in Volume II of the *Obras completas de Don Juan Donoso Cortés*, edited by Juan Juretschke (Madrid: Biblioteca de Autores Cristianos, 1946) as well as in Volume II of the *Obras completas de Donoso Cortés,* edited by Carlos Valverde (Madrid: Biblioteca de Autores Cristianos, 1970).

I have tried to capture the eloquence of Donoso's speech. His style of writing and speaking can be described as elegant and Rococo and is often difficult to render into an equally elegant English. It is full of rhetorical flourishes, very long sentences, hyperbole, rigorous logic, and colorful metaphors that are common to the Spanish of his time. For the sake of clarity I have broken many of his long sentences into smaller ones without trying to lose any of the lucidity of his thought or elegance of his speech.

A further testimony to Donoso's eloquence is his use of passages from the Latin Vulgate Bible. In these translations I have dispensed with the Latin, which appears in the Spanish original, and employed translations from the Douay-Rheims Bible, which is the closest in tone and quality to the Vulgate.

Return to the Middle Ages, to primitive mentality, to the soil, to religion, to the arsenal of worn-out solutions. To grant a shadow of efficacy to those panaceas, we should have to act as if our acquired knowledge had ceased to exist, as if we had learned nothing, and pretend in short to erase what is inerasable. We should have to cancel the contribution of several centuries and the incontrovertible acquisitions of a mind that has finally (in its last step forward) re-created chaos on its own. That is impossible. In order to be cured, we must make peace with this lucidity, this clairvoyance. We must take into account the glimpses we have suddenly had of our exile. Intelligence is in confusion not because knowledge has changed everything. It is so because it cannot accept that change. It hasn't "got accustomed to that idea." When this does happen, the confusion will disappear. Nothing will remain but the change and the clear knowledge that the mind has of it. There's a whole civilization to be reconstructed.

—Albert Camus

Introduction: Juan Donoso Cortés and the Philosophy of Counterrevolution

THE SECOND GENERATION OF REACTION

In recent years there has been increased interest in the ideas of the German legal and political theorist Carl Schmitt. Schmitt was committed to a particular worldview that was authoritarian and conservative. He was part of what can be called the "third generation" of reaction against the revolutionary movements within Western civilization that began with the French Revolution. These generations of reaction correspond to the three generations of revolution—first generation: the Enlightenment and the French Revolution; second generation: the European revolutions of 1848; and the third generation: the Russian Revolution. Joseph de Maistre and Louis de Bonald are among the chief theorists of the "first generation" of reaction.

The revolutions that rocked Europe in 1848 gave rise to a reaction that was well represented by the Spanish thinker, statesman, and diplomat Juan Donoso Cortés (1809–1853).[1] Donoso reacted against the revolutions of 1848 in the same way that de Maistre and de Bonald reacted against the Enlightenment and the French Revolution. Just as the movement towards liberalism and secularism had its *philosophes*, such as Voltaire, Rousseau, Locke, and Montesquieu, so the movement of counterrevolution and reaction also had its *contre-philosophes*.

De Maistre and de Bonald were the earliest and most important of the counterrevolutionary *philosophes*.[2] In their works they sought to provide eloquent and convincing philosophical arguments justifying the restoration and maintenance of the *ancien régime* in France and the rest of Europe. But they went even further in claiming that their vision of that régime was a model for all civilization. They advocated the restoration of what they considered to be the pinnacle of all civilization—the Christian Middle Ages, or Christendom. De Maistre and de Bonald saw the rise of liberalism and secularism, epitomized by the French

Revolution, as the destruction of that medieval "Christian" order of civilization. They wanted to restore Christendom, an order of civilization with the Pope of Rome as the supreme head and ruler, both spiritually and temporally, and the various monarchs and ecclesiastics ruling in their kingdoms and dioceses as papal vassals. The pope was considered to be the spiritual and temporal vicar of God on earth, while the monarchs were the temporal vicars and the bishops the spiritual vicars of the pope. All authority to exercise power and rule in matters spiritual and temporal came directly from God and rested in his vicar on earth, the pope. Bishops and monarchs were merely considered to be papal deputies ruling their subjects in the name of God at the sufferance of the pope.

God was said to be the ultimate sovereign of this order of civilization ruling through the pope and his deputies.[3] Any revolt against this order and the authorities and institutions maintaining it was declared a revolt against God, a slide down the "slippery slope" of liberalism and secularism into an abyss of godlessness. Liberalism and secularism represented the revolutionary annihilation of Christendom as well as the perdition of human beings.

The ideas of de Maistre and de Bonald were kept alive by Donoso as he struggled to craft a coherent ideological response calculated to roll back the revolutionary tide. That revolutionary tide was represented in his generation by the ideologies of liberalism and socialism. The counter-ideology was called "Catholicism" by Donoso. Like de Maistre and de Bonald before him, Donoso saw Catholicism as a conservative bulwark defending Christian civilization against what he viewed as the scourge of revolutionary barbarism and annihilation.

The years of Donoso's counterrevolutionary activity span from 1848 to 1853, the year of his death. During that time he produced one major work, his *Ensayo sobre el catolicismo, el liberalismo y el socialismo* (*Essay on Catholicism, Liberalism, and Socialism*), delivered some highly publicized speeches in the Cortes, and wrote a number of important letters to some of the most influential figures of his time. Even though he may have been somewhat forgotten after his death, his *Ensayo*, speeches, and letters had a major impact at the time and continued to influence conservative and Catholic thought for over a century.

During the 1920s Schmitt brought renewed attention to Donoso's thought. In the face of the political and social instability that plagued the Weimar Republic in the early 1920s, Schmitt developed a theory of sovereignty that borrows heavily from Donoso. The ideas contained in Donoso's theory of dictatorship are reflected in Schmitt's works *Political Theology* and *The Concept of the Political*.[4] Furthermore, Schmitt's notion of the friend/ enemy dichotomy, which he developed in *The Concept of the Political*, bears a resemblance to Donoso's vision of the world as a battleground between good and evil.[5]

In *The Anatomy of Antiliberalism* Stephen Holmes dedicates a chapter to Schmitt.[6] Holmes does acknowledge Hobbes' influence on Schmitt. However, there is a major lacuna in Holmes' discussion of Schmitt. Holmes never mentions Donoso and his influence upon Schmitt. This is odd considering the fact that Schmitt wrote an entire book about Donoso[7] and has a chapter about him (along with de Maistre and de Bonald) in his *Political Theology*.[8] While presenting us with a masterful discussion of de Maistre, Holmes overlooks a major influence upon Schmitt and thus presents us with an incomplete picture of the German thinker. John McCormick, in his recently published work on Schmitt,[9] does acknowledge the importance of Donoso's thought on Schmitt, but does not go into any great detail on the matter. Donoso's contribution to Schmitt's thought cannot be overlooked, overemphasized, or ignored. Donoso's influence on Schmitt can be seen in the latter's anthropology, in his theory on sovereignty, and in his critique of parliamentary democracy.

Donoso's vision of what he called "Catholic civilization" was the model of Catholicism embraced by the Franco régime (1936–1975) as a central element of its ideological justification.[10] We can also see resonances of Donoso's thought in the fascist régime of Mussolini in Italy as well as the conservative authoritarian régimes of Salazar in Portugal (1932–1968), Pétain in France (the Vichy régime, 1940–1944), and Dollfuss and Schuschnigg in Austria (1933–1938).[11] All of these régimes relied upon a certain vision of Catholicism in order to provide legitimacy and gain support for themselves. The conservative authoritarian régimes, presenting themselves as bulwarks of Western and Christian civilization by defending it from liberalism and communism, favored Catholicism and embraced a certain vision of it as an essential pillar of civilization.[12]

These régimes came into existence in response to national crises which were resolved by the use of extraordinary and extralegal means. The crises served as the justification for the seizure of power and the implementation of dictatorial governments. In each of these cases the normal institutional and legal structures and means were seen as impotent in the face of the mortal threat of revolution and social disintegration. Disintegrating force could only be met with an integrating counterforce. The revolutionary violence of socialists and communists could only be met with the counterrevolutionary violence of conservatives and fascists. A dictatorship of the proletariat could only be prevented by a dictatorship of a *Führer*, a *Duce*, or a *Caudillo*. Donoso's theory of dictatorship is among the principle explanations for this counterrevolutionary notion of dictatorship. Like Schmitt in the early twentieth century, he provides a rigorous theoretical framework justifying dictatorship.

Donoso's thought also had an influence on the dictatorial régime of Louis Napoleon (1850–1871) in France. Catholics like Donoso and his close friend Louis Veuillot[13] enthusiastically supported the French dictatorship, which is often referred to as "protofascist."[14] It was the model and precursor for later fascist and "semi-fascist" régimes. Donoso was a confidante of Louis Napoleon[15] while he was the Spanish ambassador to France in the 1850s until his death in Paris in 1853. It was during this time that he published the *Ensayo*. Furthermore, his *Speech on Dictatorship* was published in French and widely distributed in France at that time.

VILE HUMANITY

Donoso's view of humanity is rather dark and pessimistic. From his "Catholic" perspective, Donoso, heavily influenced by de Maistre,[16] sees the world and human beings as essentially corrupt and evil and therefore in need of repressive mechanisms of control and imposed dogmatic explanations of "reality." The need for dogma implicitly reveals the notion that the cosmos is unintelligible to human reason and therefore needs to be understood by means of explanations promulgated by authorities held to be infallible. Human reason is considered by Donoso to be so corrupt that it cannot be trusted to discern or explain anything. Thus it is dependent upon the pronouncements of an authority that is believed to be unerring.

Such a stance implies that the cosmos is meaningless to human beings, or that human reason is so helpless that it cannot connect with anything intelligible in the cosmos and discern meaning through the exercise of critical thought. Only through the dictatorial imposition of dogmatic explanations can it make any sense, according to Donoso. The cosmos is intelligible and has meaning only through the dogmas concocted and imposed by those wielding nfallible authority. And the human will is so weak and vile that human beings must be tamed and controlled by sovereigns wielding oppressive dictatorial authority. Donoso's Catholicism is a totalitarian system that explains all things through its dogmas and rules by means of the exercise of dictatorial authority.

There is, however, something more ominous in this. Donoso's dictatorial dogmatism reflects a spiritual emptiness that is so prevalent in the contemporary world. A world that lacks spiritual depth and integrity is a dangerous place where empty people tend to gravitate toward whatever promises to fill their void with answers and gives them a sense of rootedness and security. Donoso's dictatorial dogmatism is a perfect example of this tragic dynamic.

This dogmatism, though, does not overcome the emptiness, but only mitigates it. The spiritually empty person must believe in something, in anything, to cope with the often disconcerting, complex, inconvenient, and terrifying realities of human existence. Thus faith becomes a desperate clinging of empty people to something that provides them a modicum of security and a sense of belonging in a tenuous cosmos. Czeslaw Milosz observes, "Today man believes there is *nothing* in him, so he accepts *anything*, even if he knows it to be bad, in order to find himself at one with others, in order not to be alone."[17] It is best to believe something, to cling to something, than to believe in or cling to nothing. Belief in something at least accomplishes the purpose of situating a person in a secure and recognizable place.

Dogmatic explanations, regardless of their truth value or the quality of their reasons, can be very useful and effective in explaining the world and situating a person in it. "A world that can be explained even with bad reasons is a familiar world."[18] In this way, faith is transformed into what Albert Camus describes as "philosophical suicide" whereby we are swallowed up by a unifying principle we impose upon our consciousness in order to cope with the vicissitudes of the world.[19]

This will to believe is also ominous because it makes people malleable to the unscrupulous designs of those who are hungry for power over their fellow human beings. "The greatest temptation of human history," notes Nicolai Berdyaev, "is the temptation to exercise sovereignty and in it is concealed a most powerful enslaving force. . . . The whole disquieting and tangled problem of sovereignty is bound up with the fact that man has a natural disposition to dominate others."[20] This domination is a violation wreaked upon others. Since human beings also have a natural disposition to throw off the yoke of domination, ways must be found to effectively impose and maintain it. The use of terror and brute force are the most obvious means for this, as Machiavelli points out.[21] However, the use of these methods alone is most precarious due to the enormous physical effort and economic resources that must be expended. The exclusive reliance upon terror and brute force eventually wears down and exhausts the physical and economic resources of the sovereign power. Other means, therefore, must be employed in order to maintain the power of the sovereign.

A solution to this dilemma is found in the "useful falsehoods," such as the Myth of the Metals in Plato's *Republic*, and in de Maistre's "prejudices."[22] Subjects need to be persuaded or conditioned to think that their station and lot in life and society are good and proper. Religious myths and ideological systems can serve this purpose. They mystify subjects in such a way that they are reconciled and resigned to their servile condition through rituals that inspire awe, dogmatic formulas that provide certainty, myths that supply explanations and captivate the imagination, and rationalizations that justify. Especially effective in this drama of human domination has been the claim of divine sanction. This claim has been one of the most powerful and enduring methods used to mystify subjugated people into a state of passivity, resignation, and subservience. People need to be convinced and persuaded as well as coerced into servility.

The European Enlightenment represented a movement away from this servile state. The irrationality and ignorance that perpetuated this state of domination was challenged by emancipated human reason. Free-thinking persons began to arrive at different conclusions about sovereignty and the ways they should individually as well as socially organize their lives. De Maistre and Donoso sought to roll back and defeat this challenge. They depict human beings as impotent and dangerous creatures that are essentially irrational, prone to error, and morally depraved. They paint a dark and pessimistic picture of human nature in order to justify a particular system of domination. This is especially reflected and developed in their ideas on infallible authority.

INFALLIBILITY

Donoso's ideas on the notion of infallibility are a logical conclusion to his understanding of human nature as well as a cornerstone of his political and religious theories. Here we see how his thought influenced another influential player in the European power structure—the Roman Catholic Church. In the heated controversy that followed the publication of the *Ensayo*, Pope Pius IX intervened in favor of Donoso and his theories. Not only did the pope endorse Donoso's ideas, his papal régime reflected them.

In a letter to the papal nuncio in France, Raffaello Cardinal Fornari, Donoso lists what he sees as the principle errors of his times, errors calling for total condemnation. In this letter Donoso defends the temporal power of the papacy specifically in the form of political sovereignty over the Papal States. He also expresses his faith in what he identifies as the infallible authority of the Roman pontiff. The *Letter to Cardinal Fornari on the Errors of Our Times* was a precursor to Pius IX's encyclical letter *Quanta cura* and the *Syllabus of Errors*[23] and reflects the ideological momentum that culminated in the formal promulgation of the doctrine of papal infallibility. Donoso's theory of infallibility is based upon de Maistre's notion of it. It is essentially a recapitulation of de Maistre's ideas on the subject. For both de Maistre and Donoso, the fact that one exercises authority makes one infallible. To be infallible is to be incapable of erring. Therefore, to be in authority is to be incapable of erring. There is no need to be authentic, that is, intelligent, attentive, reasonable, and responsible.[24] Within such an understanding of authority, the notion of authenticity is irrelevant. Notions like authenticity can only spread doubt and confusion due to their precarious nature. But this is a reflection of the precarious nature of life itself. Yet according to Donoso's understanding, authority can only exist and be properly exercised when it is considered to be free from error.

In this way Donoso ignores the precarious nature of life by imposing upon it an authority that is seen as free of this fragility. Thus free of this precarious nature, authority can be depicted as some sort of superior entity or quality free from error. Since it is free from error, it can never be questioned or challenged in any way. The existence and proper exercise of authority entails a freedom from error on the part of anyone exercising it. Infallibility guarantees the existence and proper exercise of authority. Authority presupposes infallibility; to be in authority means to be infallible. All social hierarchy and order as well as truth depend upon belief in and subservience to such an authority.

There can be no legitimate authority without infallibility. The exercise of authority is the exercise of the power of infallibility. Governance is the exercise of the infallible authority to command. This same authority is the foundation for truth. Truth is found through faith, which is an unquestioning adherence to doctrines in obedience to those authorities teaching and maintaining them. These authorities must be obeyed because they are infallible. Infallibility and authority are essentially two different ways to express the same reality. De Maistre writes:

Infallibility in the spiritual order and *sovereignty* in the temporal order are two perfectly synonymous words. The one and the other explain that high power which dominates everything, from which all things are derived, which governs and is not governed, which judges and is not judged.

When we say that *the Church is infallible*, it is well essential to observe that we do not demand any particular privilege for it. We only demand that it enjoy the common right of all possible sovereignties which necessarily act as infallible, because every government is absolute. From the moment it can be resisted under the pretext of error or injustice it no longer exists.[25]

This notion of infallibility embraced by de Maistre and Donoso contributed to preparing the ground for the declaration of papal infallibility in 1870 during the First Vatican Council.[26] That declaration was one of the most significant events in an era dominated by a dictatorial authoritarian régime headed by the pope within the Roman Church that was to last until the advent of the Second Vatican Council. This régime was established in reaction against the revolution in 1848 (when the pope was forced to flee revolutionary mobs in Rome), the Italian unification in 1871 (when the Papal States were seized and incorporated into a secular Italian state), and the ideological challenges posed to the Church by liberalism and socialism. The extraordinary circumstances of these events and challenges provided the justification for the papacy to take exceptional measures in the quest to restore order. The establishment of a centralized and dictatorial authoritarian régime under the pope was the exceptional means taken by the Church to accomplish this restoration.[27] The pope was seen as the supreme head of the Church—all power and authority emanated from him through the hierarchically structured ecclesiastical functionaries, that is, through the cardinals, archbishops, bishops, presbyters, and deacons. In this way Pius IX, deeply influenced by Donoso's ideas, restructured the Church so that it would be able to wage a total war against the modern world.[28]

All power was consolidated in the person of the pope and the Vatican bureaucracy. Many new religious orders for men and women were founded while some of the older orders, like the Jesuits and Dominicans, dramatically increased in size. Seminaries were founded in Rome for every major national group. The idea behind these seminaries was to instill the "Roman spirit" in the clergy. These seminaries became the training grounds for most of the diocesan bishops around the world, serving the process of consolidation and centralization of power, making papal functionaries out of them. As societies became more secularized, the authoritarian papal régime gained in strength over the Church in an effort to counter the secular advances in the world. The Church, characterized by "its strict adherence to a papally endowed hierarchy of authority,"[29] came to be seen as another power in the war against liberalism, socialism, and atheistic communism.

We cannot adequately comprehend the history of the Roman Church from 1789 to 1960 without being thoroughly acquainted with Donoso's notion of Catholicism and his theory of infallibility. With the establishment of a dictatorial authoritarian papal régime came a systematic campaign to stamp out all voices of dissent within the Church. Just as the other dictatorial régimes could not tolerate dissent, the Church also could not tolerate it. Every step had to be taken to silence those voices that were perceived as advocates of dissent and revolution in the Roman Church. We see this particularly in the antimodernist campaign which reached its zenith during the pontificate of Pius X (1903–1910) and continued until the Second Vatican Council (1962–1965). The Church's "crusade" against modernism resulted in the silencing and condemnation of many eminent theologians and thinkers—as, for example, Friedrich von Hügel, George Tyrrell, and Alfred Loisy[30]—and helped to establish a "ghetto" or "bunker" existence calculated to shield Catholics and the Church from a hostile outer world.

THE IDEOLOGICAL JUSTIFICATION OF PANIC

Resonances of Donoso's ideas can not only be found in the theology and practices of the Roman Church and in theories of Carl Schmitt, but also in the conservative counterrevolutionary movement, or "conservative revolution," that culminated in the rise of fascism in the early twentieth century. Edgar Jung describes the conservative revolution as

> the return to respect for all those elementary laws and values without which the individual is alienated from nature and God. . . . In the place of equality comes the inner value of the individual; in the place of socialist convictions, the just integration of people into their place in a society of rank; in place of mechanical selection, the organic growth of leadership; in place of bureaucratic compulsion, the inner responsibility of genuine self-governance; in place of mass happiness, the right of the personality formed by the nation.[31]

The conservative revolutionary movement provided many of the essential themes against liberal democracy that were appropriated and then radicalized by the fascists in Spain, Italy, and Germany.[32] In the case of Germany, a number of influential theorists who lamented the state of the Weimar Republic saw the resolution of Germany's problems "not in the restoration of the monarchy, but in the founding of a new type of dynamic authoritarian *Reich* to replace and harness national energies."[33]

Donoso was a key figure in the trajectory of counterrevolutionary and authoritarian conservative thought, forming a pivotal link in the progression of that thought from de Maistre to Schmitt,[34] the conservative revolution, and fascism.[35] The political and social vision that Donoso enunciated in his final years was a synthesis of a number of perspectives. It combined the historical perspectives of Vico, de Maistre, and Hegel, the metaphysics of Plato, Aristotle, Augustine, and Aquinas, and the anthropology of Augustine, Machiavelli, Hobbes, Calvin, and de Maistre.[36] This vision is most clearly spelled out in his *Speech on Dictatorship*, *Speech on the Situation in Europe*, the *Ensayo*, and various letters to eminent political and ecclesiastical figures. The synthesis worked out by Donoso in these works put him in a unique position among authoritarian conservative thinkers. It is a synthesis in which he uses a few ideas from Augustine and some modern thinkers to restate and employ anew the ideas of de Maistre in his own time.

He was unique in the sense that he contributed significantly to establishing the vocabulary, tone, and mood of counterrevolutionary thought for more than a century. Donoso provided much of the vocabulary that was used by Pius IX in the *Syllabus of Errors* and by various authoritarian conservatives as well as fascists. He contributed in a major way in setting the tone through an æsthetically alluring, logically rigorous, and eloquent presentation of the authoritarian conservative position. He attempted to create a mood of apocalyptic terror and despair, reflecting the panic of many in the face of social and political change. In fact, Donoso's ideology can be seen as a form of rationalized panic. Many panic in the face of change and the messiness that is a natural part of human lives and institutions. Motivated by panic, enemies are sought out so that blame can be assessed and a focus of reaction and activity can be provided. These enemies can be imagined as well as real. It makes no essential difference. What is crucial, though, is that an enemy—a straw man or scapegoat—be found or invented. The creation of straw men and scapegoats, as Donoso made of Proudhon,[37] is an integral part of what can be called an *epistemology of panic*. This is an attempt to formulate a systematic rationalization of one's own terror. Rather than confront the reality of a situation or position, it is easier to form a caricature that conforms to some sort of ideology or set of preconceived notions which serve as a façade for some other agenda or phenomenon, like panic. But it can be said that the very nature of a reactionary is to be someone in panic.[38]

Paulo Freire provides a poignant description of many of the elements that comprise this phenomenon. Within any society that is experienced as "closed," a certain alienation is experienced by many, if not most, of that society's members. In a closed society people adapt themselves as objects within an environment that is shut to the hope and possibility of change. Closed societies are seen as finished, as complete systems, just as Donoso described Catholicism to be "a complete system of civilization."[39] They are closed to dialogue because that implies an incompleteness to the system. If a system is complete, it requires no change. Only that which is incomplete has the potential and need for change. What is complete has no such potential or need. It is a *fait accompli*. It cannot change. If it cannot change, and if it requires and needs no change, it is not in need of critical analysis. Dialogue is unnecessary if critical analysis is not required, because dialogue involves an interactive discussion between those holding differing critical viewpoints in an effort to reach a consensus. However, since the system is complete, all that is necessary is a passive acquiescence to those in authority, who are its infallible guardians.

Those who are ruled are governed by decree and remain silent before the voice of the master or authority. The ruled have no sense of personal or civic responsibility. They follow and obey the voice of authority; they adapt to the conditions set by those who dominate them. Open societies are seen as unfinished, incomplete. They are therefore open to critical analysis, development, and transformation based upon the liberal democratic notion of dialogue among citizens who have a sense of personal and civic responsibility.[40]

THE ORIGINS OF FASCISM

Isaiah Berlin describes Joseph de Maistre as

> a Catholic reactionary, a scholar and an aristocrat . . . outraged alike by the doctrines and acts of the French Revolution, opposed with equal firmness to rationalism and empiricism, liberalism, technocracy and egalitarian democracy, hostile to secularism and all forms of non-denominational, non-institutionalized religion, a powerful, retrograde figure, deriving his faith and his method from the Church Fathers and the teaching of the Jesuit order. "A fierce absolutist, a furious theocrat . . . always and everywhere the champion of the hardest, narrowest, most inflexible dogmatism, a dark figure out of the Middle Ages, part learned doctor, part inquisitor, part executioner." He is a Roman of the fifth century, baptized, but Roman; or alternatively a "Prætorian of the Vatican."[41]

What is said here about de Maistre can equally be said about Donoso. Berlin has something else to say about de Maistre that is also applicable to Donoso when he states that "Maistre may have spoken the language of the past, but the content of what he had to say presaged the future."[42] It would not be inaccurate to describe Donoso as a Spanish de Maistre. Donoso inherited the mantle from de Maistre as the champion *par excellence* of the reactionary and authoritarian conservative cause. His defense of dictatorship and strong infallible authority contributed to preparing the ground, both spiritually and ideologically, for the rise of fascism in the twentieth century.

When examining the ideas of de Maistre and Donoso we are looking at the ideological origins of fascism.[43] We are also examining something that can be seen as a kind of spiritual despair which is the foundation of panic, ideological dogmatism, and political as well as religious dictatorship. Fascism emerged from an ideological and cultural context grounded in irrational authoritarianism. In such a context, authority is unconditionally respected and obeyed. Critical thinking and dissent are suppressed. And disobedience is considered one of the worst offenses anyone can commit.[44]

Particularly prominent in European thinking at the end of the nineteenth century was the notion that Western civilization was in a state of decline or failure.

In this milieu grew a myth that became a primary focus of emphasis with conservative as well as fascist thinkers.[45] Roger Griffin identifies this as the "myth of *decadence*."[46] A wide range of religious, nationalist, and social movements, of a nature ranging from authoritarian conservative to fascist, emerged throughout Europe seeking to overcome the decadence through programs promising "restoration" and "regeneration."[47] Donoso is a prominent figure in this development since he was one of the first thinkers to introduce and popularize the theme of decadence. His theory of dictatorship emerges as his specific remedy for a civilization in decline. So he not only was the harbinger of a shift of emphasis in the counterrevolutionary movement away from monarchical legitimacy to dictatorship, he was also among the earliest voices contributing to the emergence of the myth of decadence. This theme is prominent in his *Speech on Dictatorship*, *Letters to the Count of Montalembert*, *Speech on the Situation in Europe*, *Letter to Queen María Cristina*, and the *Letter to Cardinal Fornari on the Errors of Our Times*. This is why he stands out in the minds of some as a Cassandra-like prophet of doom in the nineteenth century.[48]

It is important that we study the ideas of Donoso in the same way that we study the ideas of other authoritarian conservative thinkers like Joseph de Maistre, Ramiro de Maeztu, Charles Maurras, Charles Peguy, Ernst Jünger, Carl Schmitt, Henri Massis, Alain de Benoist, and T. S. Eliot as well as fascist thinkers like Giovanni Gentile, Gabriele D'Annunzio, José Antonio Primo de Rivera, and Mussolini.[49] While we can distinguish between authoritarian conservatism and fascism, we must nevertheless see these two ideologies sharing similar world views, since they come from the same philosophical and spiritual roots in reaction against the same phenomena.

Among these common roots are: (1) A contempt for the rationalism of the Enlightenment and the revolutions it inspired, owing to a view of human nature as essentially corrupt; (2) Elitism exhibiting itself in feelings and expressions of superiority of "us" over "them" and opposition to the principles of social and political equality. Here we encounter such phenomena as racism, classism, sexism, nationalism, religious triumphalism, ideological sectarianism, and tribalism; (3) An ideological intransigence expressing itself through some form of dogmatic orthodoxy and hostility to rational discussion or dialogue. Such notions as "socialist realism," the "absolute," "Catholic Truth," "National Socialist ardor," or "eternal verities" exemplify this absolutist tendency to claim that "we have all the answers"; (4) The myth of decadence which manifests itself in portraying civilization in a state of decline and decay; (5) Belief in a hierarchical social order; (6) Belief in the primacy of authority and obedience; (7) Opposition to liberalism,[50] socialism, and communism; (8) The desire to restore some mythic status or past that has been lost, such as racial purity, "traditional values," empire, or national glory, to name a few; (9) A need for scapegoats and enemies; (10) Hostility to critical thinking resulting in suspicion of, and "witch hunts" against, elements depicted as unorthodox, decadent, and subversive, like artists and intellectuals; (11) Emphasis on community, group, and institutions over and against individuals and their rights; conformity and unity, not diversity and pluralism.

Fascism differs from authoritarian conservatism in its more populist appeal and its futuristic orientation. Authoritarian conservatism appeals more to traditional and established social élites and emphasizes the preservation or restoration of the social and political orders that have sustained their privileged status. Fascism tends to appeal to the less privileged classes and seeks to create a "New Man." Authoritarian conservatism is also more religious in scope, while fascism is more secular. However, the fascism of the Legionnaire movement in Romania was thoroughly grounded in religion.[51] There were also strong religious influences in the fascism of the *Falange* in Spain.[52] Nevertheless, while fascism may be more radical than conservative in terms of its ultimate agenda and appeal, both stand together in their opposition to certain trends in the modern world. Fascism, building upon a critique of modernity and nostalgia it shares with authoritarian conservatism, is a radical culmination of that conservatism. Mark Neocleous describes it this way:

> Fascism is the end-point of reactionary counterrevolutionary thought against the Enlightenment, realized in the radically altered political conditions of the twentieth century. Being a movement of modernity, for modernity, and yet against the emancipatory potential of modernity, fascist reactionary modernism mobilizes the masses against themselves. It captures the human desire for a different—and radically better—world but, abandoning the political and philosophical project of Enlightenment and emancipation, it refuses to let rationalization become truly rational.[53]

It is my contention, however, that whatever differences there are between authoritarian conservatism and fascism, they have shown themselves to be minor. They have much more in common, which is shown by the fact that fascists and conservatives have rarely hesitated to collaborate in pursuit of common goals and in opposition to common enemies. The Italian fascists and German National Socialists could have never arrived at and remained in power without the collaboration of conservative elements in their respective countries. And the authoritarian conservative régimes of Franco in Spain, Salazar in Portugal, Pétain in France, Horthy in Hungary, Dollfuss and Schuschnigg in Austria, and Antonescu in Romania relied upon the support of fascists in varying degrees. This suggests an ideological affinity between fascism and conservatism based upon common roots and antipathies that emerged in the nineteenth century.

Donoso's thought is a key expression of those principles that form the link between these two ideological currents. The theory that Donoso developed, permitting a shift of authoritarian conservatism away from an exclusive emphasis on the restoration of order under the monarchical *ancien régime* to an emphasis on the restoration of order by non-monarchical means, resonates in the ideas emanating from the German conservative revolution against the Weimar Republic as well as in the authoritarian conservative régimes that came to power in the 1920s, 1930s, and 1940s.

THE THEORY OF DICTATORSHIP

Donoso, like Schmitt, sees human beings as evil in the sense that they are dangerous.[54] Both Donoso and Schmitt were responding to similar political and social crises of an exceptional character. These crises were exceptional because the traditional and normal institutional structures—namely monarchies, parliaments, and laws—were impotent before the particular exigencies that emerged in Europe during and after the revolutions of 1848 and in Germany during the early years of the Weimar Republic. Donoso and Schmitt saw that exceptional political and social situations call for exceptional solutions, that is, solutions outside the normal body of constitutional laws.[55] It is the responsibility of the sovereign of a community to decide *when* such an exceptional situation exists, *that* such a situation exists, *how* sovereignty is to be exercised in that situation, and *how long* that exceptional mode of sovereignty is to be exercised.

The basis for this understanding of sovereignty is the realization that no institution or body of laws can foresee every contingency that can emerge within a political community. Thus there are going to be situations arising which cannot be dealt with through the regular institutional and legal channels. Nevertheless, decisions must be made in such circumstances. Therefore, for both Donoso and Schmitt, some form of exceptional rule, namely dictatorship, becomes necessary in these exceptional situations.[56] In the circumstances in which both Donoso and Schmitt found themselves, the traditional monarchies had been overthrown and the parliaments and laws that replaced them were seen by them to be impotent. In particular, Donoso and Schmitt saw the parliaments of their respective times and settings as discussion clubs, places where endless debates take place and where little or nothing is ever decided. For Donoso and Schmitt, exceptional social and political circumstances call for decisions, not discussions.[57] Discussions just lead to ever more discussions. They resolve absolutely nothing.

This line of thinking can be traced back to de Maistre. In this regard Stephen Holmes writes about de Maistre:

> Liberal theorists are deluded: "they brag of their enlightenment, but they know nothing because they do not know themselves." They fatuously believe that human beings are naturally good. This is why they deny the absolute necessity of a divinely sanctioned authority to punish wicked humanity and keep it under control. But there is no thesis more frequently confirmed by experience than the ineradicability of original sin. Man was born evil and remains so. . . . Such incurably corrupt creatures cannot be perfected, or even bettered, by enlightenment and secular education. They must be brought to heel. They cannot live without an unlimited ruler whose decisions are beyond dispute.[58]

Again, what is said here about de Maistre can also be said about Donoso. Both of them held that if human beings are essentially corrupt and depraved and drawn to error and absurdity, then they are incapable of reaching any level of enlightenment that would enable them to enter into rational discussion and arrive at a consensus concerning the best way to live. For both Donoso and de Maistre rationalist "enlightenment" precipitates a questioning process that undermines all respect for authority, thus leading to social chaos and disintegration. For Donoso some kind of repressive mechanism is necessary in order to avoid this. That mechanism is dictatorship.

> it was [Donoso] Cortés who recognized that the religious and national conservative powers in Europe—Catholic royalty in its Romance form, the dynastic character of evangelical Prussia, and the partnership of Russian orthodoxy with czarism—were doomed: they would never, in his judgment, be able to achieve the same homogeneous unity that marked for him the movement of "international" revolution. In view of this overwhelmingly likely development, Cortés was convinced that there was only one avenue of escape: dictatorship.[59]

Donoso, like de Maistre, was an ardent monarchist. Monarchy, for him, was as natural for society as the patriarchal family is for individuals. However, corruption and depravity are also natural for society as well as for individuals. Sometimes situations arise within societies, exceptional situations, that can overwhelm the capacity of normal and legal institutional structures to deal with them. These exceptional situations constitute a breakdown of social and political order. In such cases exceptional measures need to be taken so that order can be restored because there are truths that Donoso sees as eternal which do not allow human beings to exist in a void.[60] Human beings require the discipline of order and the absolute certainty of beliefs to avoid a rootless, ephemeral, and indecisive existence. All situations, especially exceptional ones, demand a disciplined decisiveness to overcome them.

An exceptional situation consists of two elements: (1) corruption of the social and political order and (2) corruption of the governmental institutions upon which the social and political order depends. In such a situation subversive forces, like socialism, are dominant unless they are countered by some superior force on the side of order.[61] A corrupt monarchy cannot restore order to a corrupt society. Therefore some extrainstitutional means must be taken so that order can be restored. Donoso posits dictatorship as the extrainstitutional way to restore order.[62] "When the letter of the law is enough to save a society, then the letter of the law is best. But when it is not enough, then dictatorship is best."[63]

This key distinction is the most important contribution Donoso made in the development of the counterrevolutionary ideological trajectory that started with the monarchical restorationism of de Maistre and de Bonald and culminated in fascism. *How* authority is exercised became more important than *what form* that authority takes. Ultimately it does not matter whether the authority is based upon traditional modes and orders, like monarchy or a military dictatorship. What really matters is the maintenance of order in society by means of whatever form of repressive action is required. Order, therefore, is more important than any particular institutional form since the purpose of political institutions is to maintain order. If that order cannot be maintained by means of traditions, laws, or monarchs, then it must be maintained by some more radical, severe, and authoritarian means.

The door was thus opened for the emergence and development of a reactionary and counterrevolutionary ideology not bent on the restoration of the *ancien régime* but still dedicated to the restoration and maintenance of hierarchical order in society through the decisionistic—willful and decisive—exercise of authority. The end—order—justifies the means used to achieve and maintain it. Donoso justifies dictatorship as the remedy for a body politic that is diseased. When a society is in a state of "advanced disease," dictatorship is the only remedy that can save it from succumbing.

Donoso considers dictatorship to be a theoretically correct form of government, as demonstrated by history as well as by God. Just as exceptional circumstances in the natural order require exceptional means to remedy them, so in the political order exceptional circumstances require analogous exceptional and decisionistic means of remedy.[64]

In exceptional circumstances in both the natural and political orders, the laws that govern these orders are inoperative. It is therefore necessary to act in a manner that goes beyond the scope and sanction of the laws, that is, to resort to exceptional means of action. In the natural order this exceptional means is called a miracle; in the political order it is called dictatorship.[65] A dictatorship is a miracle in the political order; and a miracle is dictatorship in the natural order. This is the heart of Donoso's argument justifying dictatorship. This argument resonates in Schmitt's notion of the jurisprudential exception.[66]

All authority, according to Donoso, is repressive, owing to the "radically fallen and sick" condition of human nature. A sick understanding needs to be unquestioningly obedient to an infallible authority; a sick will needs to be "repressed" by a sovereign.[67] This repression is twofold—religious and political. Religious repression is a form of internal control over a person, while political repression is external control, that is, control coming from outside that is imposed upon a person. Civilization depends for its survival upon this twofold repression. A decrease in the hold of religious repression results in an increase in political repression. To the degree that internal restraints fail to control human beings, external restraints become necessary. The fall of religious control brings about the rise of political control and tyranny. "This," Donoso says, "is a law of humanity, a law of History." Therefore, if it is necessary, dictatorship is justified as a means to keep the scales of repression tipped on the side of religion. But if it cannot be religious, then it must be political.

To understand this better we need to examine Donoso's law of equilibrium, a notion that he shares with de Maistre. The order of the cosmos consists in a certain symmetry or proportionality between all things. De Maistre equated order with proportionality: "order is nothing but *deliberate proportionality*, and symmetry nothing but *recognized and compared order*."[68] Everything is placed in a perfect and deliberate equilibrium by God. If there is a heaven, there must be a hell; if there is disorder, then there is order; if there is evil, there is good; if there is crime, there must be revenge; if there is error, there is truth; if there is a natural realm, there is a supernatural one; if there is ebb, there must be flow.[69]

This equilibrium fits into Donoso's dualistic conception of the universe. Two elements always need to remain in a certain proportion. As one element rises, the other falls proportionally. There can never be a vacuum. For example, as the influence of religion over societies declines, the influence of politics rises. So religion exists in a certain equilibrium with politics. The same argument is used by Donoso to justify dictatorships. As monarchies lose their influence over societies, dictatorships are needed to rule over them. Donoso's identification of repression with civilization has something rather Freudian about it. Both Donoso and Freud identify repression as necessary for the development and maintenance of civilization. They see that without repression, civilization can do nothing but slide into a state of barbarism in which human beings degenerate into beasts capable of destroying one another.[70] The irony in all this was that Freud was an atheist while Donoso was a fervent believer. Yet he and Donoso shared the same Hobbesian vision of human nature; they also shared the view that religion is useful for the maintenance of order and unity in society.[71]

Here we really must confront what seems to be an ambiguity in Donoso's thought. He defends the notion of dictatorship and supports his views by referring to the example of the Roman Republic. But is the dictatorship he advocates analogous to the temporary or "commisarial" nature of dictatorship during the time of the Roman Republic?

A Roman dictator received a commission for an appointed period of time to deal with a specific problem in a period of extreme emergency, that is, in exceptional circumstances. Dictators exercised unlimited powers in the specific performance of their commission. They were not restricted by any law or norm as long as they operated within the bounds of their commission; they could not permanently change or suspend the regular constitutional order. Once their task was completed within the time constraints placed upon them, they relinquished the powers relating to their specific commission to restore the regular constitutional order, not replace it.[72]

Another form of dictatorship is a "sovereign" dictatorship.[73] It is used not only to change the regular constitutional order, but is also a regular constitutional order in itself. Unlike a commisarial dictatorship, which is temporary because it is operative in exceptional circumstances that disrupt a constitutional order, a sovereign dictatorship is permanent. Such a dictatorship is analogous to Hobbes' notion of absolute sovereignty.[74]

Even though Donoso does not use this terminology to make a distinction between different types of dictatorship, he nevertheless makes this distinction.

He is aware, when he refers to the Roman dictatorship at the time of the Republic, that it amounted to a temporary suspension of the regular constitutional order because of exceptional circumstances endangering the polity. However, when he refers to the English Parliament, he describes it as exercising a permanent dictatorship. Its dictatorship was not exceptional, but permanent. It was the law; it was sovereign.

In discussing both types of dictatorship Donoso seeks to demonstrate that dictatorship is a natural and good form of government. The ambiguity emerges when we try to discern whether he advocates this as a temporary or a permanent form of government. While he cites the example of the dictatorship of the Roman Republic to support his argument, he also cites the example of the English Parliament. My view is that he favors permanent—sovereign—dictatorship because this is consistent with his Hobbesian view of human nature as something essentially dark, corrupt, and warlike.[75] For Hobbes, the natural condition of the human person is a state of war. But from the classical Roman republican perspective, a state of war is an exceptional state, not a permanent state. As exceptional, it is a state that constitutes a departure from the regular pacific order. Thus this exceptional state requires recourse to exceptional means to restore the regular pacific order. However, what was exceptional to the Romans during the time of the Republic became permanent for Hobbes. War is a permanent trait of human nature for him. Only something just as permanent can mitigate or alleviate it, a permanent and absolute sovereign exercising permanent and absolute power. Hobbes' permanent and absolute sovereign exercises the power of sovereign dictatorship.[76] This is commensurate with his view of human nature. And it is also commensurate with Donoso's view of human nature.

Dictatorship is not meant to restore a specific kind of régime per se, but to restore a specific kind of repression. From Donoso's perspective, even if the monarchy of *ancien régime* France had been restored, it would also have been dictatorial because all régimes, whether secular or ecclesiastical, are repressive. The very nature of power, whether it be political or religious, is to be repressive and, therefore, dictatorial. Thus we can speak of various forms of government as different modes of dictatorship—monarchical dictatorship, aristocratic dictatorship, ecclesiastical dictatorship, parliamentary dictatorship, military dictatorship, presidential dictatorship. All forms of government are modes of repression and are, therefore, modes of dictatorship, according to Donoso.

His identification of two different types of repression—religious and political—as permanent features in the control of human beings reinforces the argument that he is an advocate of sovereign dictatorship. For repression can be seen as dictatorial in nature. Exceptional circumstances only help to determine the mode of sovereign dictatorship, whether the dictatorship is to be monarchical, military, presidential, or otherwise. Every mode of dictatorship serves to maintain religious and political repression. As religious repression declines in its hold upon people and societies, political repression must increase, as we see in Donoso's theory of the religious/political thermometer.[77] Any change in the equilibrium between religious and political repression constitutes an exceptional circumstance requiring a change in the mode of dictatorial régime proportional to the circumstance. Whatever mode of dictatorial régime is necessary and effective in the circumstances is the mode that must be imposed. Circumstances, not fixed principles on legitimacy, dictate the character of the régime.

Concerning Donoso on this, Schmitt notes that "legitimacy no longer exists in the traditional sense. For him there was thus only one solution: dictatorship. It is the solution that Hobbes also reached by the same kind of decisionistic thinking: "*Auctoritas, non veritas, facit legem.*"[78] This is also a kind of Machiavellian pragmatism. Whatever is necessary and effective, not absolutely virtuous or traditional, is Donoso's permanent part.[79] By abandoning monarchical legitimacy as the sole guarantor of order, Donoso shows a kind of strategic flexibility that facilitates the order that can no longer be maintained by a traditional monarchy.

Within this framework the notion of the exception is not a situation constituting a disruption of a specific constitutional order that calls for exceptional means to restore that order. An exception is a disruption of the equilibrium between the religious and political repression necessary to keep corrupt, irrational, and depraved human beings under control within a political and social order. Such a disruption is reflected in the corruption of the political and social order as well as in the governmental and other institutional structures required to maintain that order. Therefore the establishment of new institutional structures becomes necessary to maintain the new repressive equilibrium that is essential to a proper political and social order. When laws or monarchies cannot preserve political and social order by maintaining the proper equilibrium of religious and political repression, other repressive modes of government become necessary. The failure of a less severe mode of dictatorship calls for the establishment of a more severe one suitable to the circumstances.

Dictatorship is a permanent part of political and social reality as a mode of repression. The only variable in this is *how* dictatorship is exercised. Varying circumstances require different modes of dictatorship corresponding to them. Thus *how* dictatorship is exercised determines the *form* it must take. This is consistent with Donoso's position that *how* political power is exercised is more important than *what form* it takes. This is the most important contribution Donoso made to authoritarian conservative thought, moving it away from an emphasis on the restoration of hierarchical order through restoration of the monarchies and other institutions of the pre–1789 *ancien régime* to the implementation of such an order through any form of government deemed necessary and useful. What continues after this strategic shift is the antiliberal and antidemocratic nature of the ideological trajectory.

One other thing needs to be noted here. Donoso's notion of civilization as ordered and hierarchical is an *organic* conception of civilization. He sees a civilization as an organism. Like all organisms, this civil organism has parts that are arrayed in a certain fixed arrangement. Those who exercise ruling authority in the civil organism are its point of political unity, the guardians of its fundamental beliefs, and the trustees of its common good. This applies especially to Donoso's conception of Catholic civilization, which he defines as "a complete system of civilization."[80]

The "organic" in relation to social relationships refers to that which is opposed to the personal. An organic conception of civilization is based on the primacy of society over the individual person. There can be no realm of the personal in an organic conception of society. The individual person is merely an organ of society, observes Berdyaev.[81] Catholicism, as already noted, is defined by Donoso as "a complete system of civilization." It is complete in the sense that it is the sole teacher and guardian of all truth regarding God, humans, and the cosmos and that it is a whole and finished society. It establishes and maintains order in all human affairs by teaching all persons their place within the hierarchy of that order. Any break with this order is an act of disobedience, which is a sin. As a hierarchical entity it is organic. "The organic interpretation of society," writes Berdyaev, "is always hierarchical."[82]

> Society is presented as though it were a personality of a higher hierarchical degree than the personality of man. But this makes man a slave. The spiritualized interpretation of the organic nature of society idealizes the reign of law in the life of society and makes it the spiritual basis of society. The reign of law acquires, as it were, a normative character. The idea of the supremacy of society over personality is to be found in de Maistre and de Bonald, it has a reactionary counterrevolutionary origin. It was inherited by Comte also, whose influence is to be seen in Charles Maurras.[83]

Like de Maistre and de Bonald, Donoso understands society as an organic unity ruled by a set of fixed and immutable laws. This organic understanding of civilization also places Donoso's thought well in that counterrevolutionary ideological trajectory that began with the reaction against the French Revolution and culminated in the rise of fascism.[84]

DUALISM

Donoso's *Letter to the Editors of "El Pais" and "El Heraldo"* was a continuation of the polemical controversy that emerged after his *Speech on Dictatorship*. In his *Letters to the Count of Montalembert*[85] and in the *Speech on the Situation in Europe*, Donoso described the world as being divided between two totally opposing camps—Catholic civilization and philosophical civilization. He identified goodness with Catholic civilization and evil with philosophical civilization. For this he was accused by many of his opponents of being a disciple of Manichæism.[86] In the *Letter to the Editors of "El Pais" and "El Heraldo,"* Donoso attempts to refute the charges that he professed a Manichæan position. Donoso constantly stresses the importance of the question of good and evil in the world. To him everyone and everything participates in the struggle between these two factors, where the good is identified with God and evil with the world. "Every word that is pronounced is either inspired by God or by the world and necessarily proclaims, implicitly or explicitly, but always clearly, the glory of the one or the triumph of the other. In this singular warfare we all fight through forced enlistment."[87]

While Donoso is critical of Manichæism, there is something of that doctrine in his own understanding of good and evil. He takes the position, like de Maistre,[88] that there is a perpetual war occurring between good and evil in the cosmos. To the degree that Donoso understands the cosmos to be dominated by a struggle between good and evil, he, like de Maistre, approaches Manichæism. But that is the extent of Manichæan influence in Donoso's thought. He does not adhere to the Manichæan position that the universe is a raging perpetual battleground between two opposing and equal gods—one good and one evil. However, he maintains that good and evil,[89] the supernatural and the natural, the divine and the human, and God and the world are in a contest in which one is destined to be victorious over the other.

What distinguishes Donoso's position from Manichæism is his understanding and explanation of the origin of evil. Evil is "the negation of the good."[90] It does not exist substantially, that is, as something in itself, but negatively, since it is merely a negation of the good; it cannot exist without the good.[91] As the negation of the good its existence is only accidental, not essential.[92] It has no positive existence of its own, but exists merely as the negation of goodness. Donoso's notion on this echoes the position of Augustine, who described evil as dependent upon goodness, as a "privation of good."[93] This was a theme reiterated by Aquinas who wrote, "A thing essentially evil cannot exist. The foundation of evil is always a good subject."[94] God is the foundation of goodness. All goodness comes from God. "God, who is the absolute good is the supreme fabricator of all good, and all he does is good."[95] Evil, therefore, cannot be divine or divine in origin. It originates in the human. "Evil comes from man and is in man," according to Donoso.[96] More precisely, evil originates in the human faculty of choice: "Evil has its origin in the use man made of the faculty of choice, which . . . constitutes the imperfection of human liberty."[97] It cannot be the work of God, since God is perfect. For Donoso, if God is the origin of any sort of evil, it is the evil that punishes humans for their sins. But this cannot be seen truly as an evil. Punishment is the providential action of God wresting good out of evil, turning something evil into something good and salvific.[98]

Aquinas makes the same argument: "Take away all evil, and much good would go with it. God's care is to bring good out of the evils which happen, not to abolish them."[99] What can be viewed as painful and evil from a human perspective can be salvific and good from a divine perspective. The very capacity of the human being to choose evil manifests God's power to obtain good out of it. This manifestation is the precise raison d'être for that capacity to choose.

Human depravity provides the opportunity for God to exercise power in dispensing justice and mercy—bringing order out of chaos, putting everything in its proper place in the hierarchical structure of a divinely created cosmos. "The supreme reason for the existence of the faculty, conceded to the creature, whereby order is converted into disorder, harmony into ferment, good into evil, is in the power that God has of converting disorder into order, ferment into harmony, and evil into good."[100]

Donoso applies this understanding of good and evil to his critique of Manichæism. He is critical of the Manichæan view of this struggle, which he claims is shared also by socialists, like Proudhon, holding that good and evil are *equal* forces entangled in an endless struggle for control of the cosmos. In his critique Donoso identified two different types of Manichæism—the ancient and the Proudhonian.

The ancient form "consists in affirming that there is one principle of good and another of evil; that these two principles are incarnate in two gods, between whom there is perpetual war."[101] The "Manichæism" of Proudhon "consists in affirming that God is the evil and man the good, that the human and the divine are two rival powers, and that the only duty of man is to conquer God, the enemy of man."[102] God is depicted as the implacable enemy of humankind, an evil tyrant to be overthrown.

Donoso asserts that both forms of Manichæism are dualistic and that they suppose a battle of opposing forces. For him the weakness in the Manichæan position is the supposition of duality in the divinity. Reason, for Donoso, even reason "unilluminated by faith," demonstrates that God either exists or does not exist. If God exists, then there is only one God. There cannot be two gods. However, if there are two gods, and they are in combat with each other, then one of them must be victorious over the other. Every battle must be resolved by one combatant definitively suppressing and defeating the other. However, this is impossible with gods because they have a "substantial and necessary existence" and therefore cannot be suppressed and defeated.[103] This provides a foundation for Donoso's decisionism.

Donoso's decisionism does not allow him to conceive of the possibility of an unending combat. It rests upon the notion that every action must reach a decisive and definite conclusion. Therefore every battle must reach such a conclusion. There can be no such thing as an inconclusive battle. Within Donoso's decisionistic mold, Manichæan dualism, not dualism per se, is an absurdity, in contradiction with itself, because it posits the notion of an inconclusive battle.[104] Donoso's own decisionism is based on a type of dualism. We see this dualism manifested in his conception of two competing and hostile civilizations, the two forms of repression, and the combat between good and evil. What he could not abide, though, was Manichæan dualism. Yet his good *contra* evil dualism demonstrates that he was not free of its influence.

Just how is the battle resolved for Donoso? He states that there are two principles governing life—the natural and the supernatural. The natural pertains to the world and all the corruption and evil attached to it. The supernatural pertains to the otherworldly and to goodness. According to Donoso, evil must always triumph in the natural realm. But in the supernatural realm, good always triumphs. Since the supernatural prevails over the natural, good prevails over evil. Evil is naturally victorious while good is supernaturally victorious. One of the ways this happens is when evil in the natural realm is converted into a supernatural goodness. The natural evil of Christ's death became the supernatural good of human redemption; the natural evil of the destructiveness of the flood in Genesis became the supernatural good of the divine punishment of sin and a strengthening of the righteous.

While evil may triumph naturally, good triumphs supernaturally and thus is ultimately victorious because the supernatural always prevails over the natural. On the social level Donoso calls this victory a "miracle." On the level of the individual person he calls it "grace." A miracle is the principle of salvation for society while grace is the principle of salvation for the individual person.

The notions of miracle and grace are not seen by Donoso as divine gifts perfecting nature, but as divine interventions meant to save corrupt and depraved human beings and their decadent societies. From Donoso's perspective, human beings, left to their own devices, are so corrupt and depraved in their intellects and wills that no good can come from them. Human beings cannot improve their lot through the use of their rational capacity. Thus they can never be just in themselves. They are just only by the grace of God, who saves them from themselves. Without some sort of divine rescue mission, human beings and their societies are hopelessly lost and damned.

THE TWO CIVILIZATIONS

Not long after Donoso delivered his *Speech on Dictatorship* it was translated into several different languages and published throughout Europe causing a considerable amount of controversy. It was very well received among conservative and Ultramontanist circles. But it was severely attacked by Catholic and secular liberals and socialists. As a public figure and spokesman for conservatism and Ultramontanism, Donoso and his views achieved a high level of notoriety and had become a lightening rod for polemical controversy. The Catholic liberal Charles-Forbes Count of Montalembert, though, was somewhat sympathetic with the views Donoso expressed, and wrote him to that effect.

In the letters addressed to Montalembert, Donoso lays out a vision of civilization that was to be further developed in 1851 in the *Ensayo.* This is his dialectical view of two intrinsically inimical civilizations—Catholic civilization and philosophical civilization. Donoso's understanding of Augustine's two cities—the city of God (*civitas Dei*) and the earthly city[105]—is reflected in this view of civilization. It is a politicization of the notion of the two cities based on his dualistic understanding of the cosmos.

Augustine held that for the human being, goodness is the love of God above all things, even to the contempt of self, while evil is the love of self above all things, even to the contempt of God. From this it follows that the human race can be divided into two great opposing camps, one that is founded upon the love of God and another founded upon the love of self. Human beings are ultimately identified by the character and orientation of their wills with respect to what they love. What they love reveals what they are. They are distinguished by the kind of love they choose. What they love determines the camp to which they belong.[106] The entire history of the human race can be explained in terms of a dialectical relationship between these two camps—the city of God and the earthly city.

It must be questioned, however, whether this notion of the two cities was developed by Augustine in order to establish a Christian doctrine of the State. Henri de Lubac sees such an interpretation as a misunderstanding of Augustine's notion. The two cities, according to de Lubac, merely represent the two loves that form the spiritual struggle within each person. There is nothing political about this. This theme of the two cities is based on the contrast between light and darkness that is found in the Gospel of John.[107] The two cities represent the "drama" that takes place within the soul of the individual person as well as the Christian community of believers struggling with the challenge of the Gospel.

> The *City of God* is not a political treatise, not even one "taken from the holy Scripture." Neither is it a "philosophy of history." For anyone who simply reads it without intending to use it for another end, that assertion becomes perfectly obvious and its truth has always been recognized by the Church's Tradition. If it must be classified, one can say . . . that it is a "theology of history." But we must be careful to specify ... that the history is the "history of salvation," which means that it is, in its twofold and collective dimension, a treatise on Christian spirituality. It can be called a "Christian drama." In it, St. Augustine . . . takes up, develops, and deepens the allegory of the "two ways" that had served to frame the first descriptions of life in conformity with the Gospel. His essential innovation . . . was to envisage spiritual combat as more than the struggle of the isolated Christian, as involving all Church members who are drawn by the Creator to become part of his City. . . . In the *City of God* we see "Babylon," incarnated first by the fallen angels and then in the sin of our first ancestry and Cain, being born and progressing in *pride.* Whereas we see "Jerusalem," founded by Christ and his disciples in accordance with the prophetic announcements and anticipation sown throughout the Old Testament, growing in *humility.* Neither the most beautiful human successes (which St. Augustine does not fail to admire as such) nor, we shall add, the most beautiful "Christian social order," the most brilliant situation of the Church in the world, has anything to do with it.[108]

However, Donoso identifies the city of God with a "Christian social order." This order, however, resembles Hobbes' *libido dominandi*,[109] the impulse to dominate. Donoso's "Christian social order" combines Hobbes' *libido dominandi* with Augustine's notion of the city of God interpreted as a political doctrine.

Yet Donoso's political interpretation of the *City of God* may not be entirely inaccurate. There is much to suggest in Augustine's actions that indicates the plausibility of such an interpretation. "Augustine," writes Paul Johnson, "was the dark genius of imperial Christianity, the ideologue of the Church–State alliance, and the fabricator of the medieval mentality."[110] This alliance was an integral part of a "totalitarian state" that used brutal measures to enforce religious orthodoxy and political unity.

> The late empire was a totalitarian state, in some ways an oriental despotism. Antinomial elements were punished with massive force. State torture, supposedly used in serious cases such as treason, was in fact employed whenever the State willed. Jerome describes horrible tortures inflicted on a woman accused of adultery. . . . Much of the terminology of the late-imperial police system passed into the language of European enforcement, through the Latin phrases of the Inquisition. Augustine was the conduit from the ancient world. Why not? he would ask. If the State used such methods for its own miserable purposes, was not the Church entitled to do the same and more for its own greater ones? He not only accepted, he became the theorist of, persecution; and his defenses were later to be those on which all defenses of the Inquisition rested.
>
> We must not imagine that Augustine was necessarily a cruel man. . . . But he insisted that the use of force in the pursuit of Christian unity, and indeed total religious conformity, was necessary, efficacious, and wholly justified. . . . [H]e used the analogy with the State, indeed appealed to the orthodoxy of the State, in necessary and perpetual alliance with the Church in the extirpation of dissidents.[111]

Given Augustine's concept of the union of Church and State, it is easy to see how his notion of the two cities could be politically interpreted by some. Augustine's notion of the two cities was recast by Donoso into a dualistic system of contradictory and conflicting camps. Donoso identifies the two camps by calling one "Catholic civilization" and the other "philosophical civilization." He equates Catholic civilization with the city of God.[112] Philosophical civilization corresponds with Augustine's earthly city. Like the two cities, the two civilizations are delineated by what they affirm and reject.[113]

Affirmation and negation represent fundamental orientations of the will that are manifestations of faith or the lack of faith. Faith, to Donoso, is a decisionistic act, a decisive and uncritical adherence to the commands and teachings of ecclesiastical officials wielding infallible authority. Faith as well as faithlessness are the essential determining factors of what is asserted or denied by individuals and communities. What is affirmed or denied by them decisively determines the quality and shape of their character. What is believed or not believed by individuals and communities plays an enormous rôle in determining who and what they are.

The structure of the relationship between the affirmative and the negative is identical to the relationship between good and evil. Just as there can be no evil without good, so there can be no negative without an affirmative. Evil is the negation of goodness; the negative is the negation of the affirmative. Since the negative is grounded in error, and error is evil, the negative must be evil. This is just another way for Donoso to express the radical differences between the two civilizations.

Catholic civilization contains everything that is good; there is absolutely no element of evil in it. It represents respect for and obedience to authority and belief in religion. Echoing the views of de Bonald, Donoso depicts philosophical civilization as totally evil; no element of goodness can be found in it. It promotes hatred for authority and religion.[114] There is something of a Manichæan flavor in this investing of complete goodness in one civilization and complete evil in the other. Since evil is the total negation of the good there can be nothing but absolute and total enmity between the two civilizations, with complete goodness on one side and complete evil on the other. These two civilizations are in a state of total war against each other in a contest to dominate individuals and societies. Politics can only be understood in terms of this war. Donoso's *Weltanschauung* is one that perceives the world as being in a state of perpetual conflict between two totally inimical forces.[115]

This view is translated into the political order by Donoso through his development of the notion of the two conflicting civilizations. Just as there can be no cosmos without conflict, so there can be no civilization without conflict. This idea is reflected in Schmitt's notion that the world of politics depends upon the existence of friends and enemies. There can be no question of compromise or consensus between the conflicting camps.

The world of politics is a world of war between the forces of light, goodness, and truth on one side, and darkness, evil, and error on the other. "A world in which the possibility of war is utterly eliminated," observes Schmitt, "a completely pacified globe, would be a world without the distinction of friend and enemy and hence a world without politics."[116] The dialectical opposition between the two civilizations is represented by two radically different anthropologies. Their views of human nature are totally at variance with one another.

The "Catholic" anthropology developed by Donoso presents human nature as "radically fallen and sick in its essence." Being in this condition, human nature needs to be subjected and repressed by God, the Church, and political authorities because, if it is left to its own devices, it can only lead the individual person into evil and error. Human beings are entirely dependent upon the fear of God, religious and political subjugation, and the infallible authority of the Church in order to attain any modicum of truth or do any degree of good.[117]

Philosophical civilization teaches that human nature is "sound and healthy." Individual persons and communities, relying upon their own potential, can attain truth and act in a good way. Through open and civil discourse, what Donoso calls "discussion," they can achieve a certain degree of access to truth and arrive at a reasonable consensus about the good. In his rejection of "parliamentarianism" Donoso unconditionally repudiates this tenet of philosophical civilization. No matter how long or short a time or how thorough it may be, no amount of discussion can achieve any good because human beings are essentially corrupt and depraved, not sound and healthy. The most that can be expected from discussion is an accumulation of errors and a paralyzing state of indecision. These views greatly influenced Schmitt's critique of parliamentary democracy in the early twentieth century.[118]

Donoso makes repression and fear the pillars upon which Catholic civilization rests. Catholic civilization tames, or holds at bay, the evil propensities of individual persons so that they can live together in some degree of peace and harmony. Philosophy promotes the idea of the autonomous person, someone who is sane, whole, and independent. As envisioned by philosophy, civilization does not function as a mechanism for taming corrupt and depraved people. Healthy people have no need for the fear of God or for repression. There is no need for anything that is infallibly and authoritatively binding upon individuals. The freedom of philosophical civilization, claims Donoso, consists in being liberated from the bonds of authority. Alienation from God is not evil. The bonds of authority, though, are evil.

For Donoso the destruction of such bonds is the same as the destruction of civilization itself. Civilization depends very much upon such bonds if it is to survive. The purity of religious and social principles, which are entirely dependent upon these bonds, is essential for the health and survival of civilization. As a "complete system of civilization," Catholicism is perfect because its religious and social principles are perfect. These principles serve as the foundation and the element of coherence for civilization. To the degree that they are upheld, taught, and believed in their purity, civilization can be maintained. But as a reality operative in history, Catholic civilization is subject to all the "imperfections and vicissitudes" that afflict all things in history. Human beings are free to reject these principles and decide to live in ways inimical to them. There is no automatic guarantee that Catholic civilization can endure. If humans trust more in themselves than in God, then it is a sure thing that Catholic civilization will fall.

With the rejection of Catholic civilization that is signified by a shift to philosophical civilization there must be a breakdown of the order and discipline necessary to maintain a society. In a way, the notion of philosophical civilization is an oxymoron, from Donoso's perspective, because philosophy is only conducive to the destruction of civilization. Without the mechanisms of repression that are found in Catholic civilization, the human race can only find itself on the road to barbarism and annihilation.

We can, however, conceive of the notion of philosophical civilization if it is seen as a set of principles opposing the principles of Catholic civilization. In this sense we are dealing with two opposite visions of civilization that are at total war with one another. Donoso considers it inevitable that, viewed naturally, Catholic civilization would be defeated by philosophical civilization. But from a supernatural perspective, Catholic civilization would defeat philosophical civilization; the city of God will prevail over the earthly city. Every period of history ends in catastrophe. However, the hand of divine providence never stops operating. Even in the midst of the worst disasters, it is a work effecting the supernatural victory of the city of God over the earthly city, of good over evil, of Catholic civilization over philosophical civilization. Only supernatural means are efficacious with regard to the evils we experience in the world. No amount of human effort can bring about any modicum of improvement in the human lot. Life in the earthly city, in philosophical civilization, is vain because it cannot rise above evil in any way. Life in the heavenly city, in Catholic civilization, cannot eliminate evil. It can, however, transform it into something morally useful and salvific in the same way that the evil of Christ's crucifixion was transformed by God into the good of redemption.[119] As long as human beings are subject to space and time, philosophical civilization will always be victorious. It is only when we move outside these parameters that the complete victory of Catholic civilization is conceivable. Until this happens, the most that can be done is to maintain some kind of political and religious mechanism of repression—a Leviathan—to secure some measure of order that will mitigate or minimize the effects of evil in the world. That is the most for which we can hope from any form of civilization. To expect anything more is to assert that the realm of the natural is superior to the realm of the supernatural. Such a notion is anathema to Donoso.

A STATIC VIEW OF REALITY

In the *Letter to Queen María Cristina* we encounter a static view of reality, especially as it pertains to society. Donoso's static view of society is authoritarian and paternalistic. Any solutions to the problems of a society can be sought only within a static, authoritarian, and paternalistic framework. There can be no envisioning of solutions outside this framework because the framework itself constitutes the bounds of both the real as well as the possible. This makes such a framework one-dimensional, that is, the one and only way that reality can be understood.[120] Even Donoso's dualism fits within the confines of this one-dimensional framework. Everything is somehow fated to be nothing more than a scenario within a static framework of reality. This is especially evident in Donoso's views on the poor and poverty. For him there are poor people, there always have been poor people, and there always will be poor people. The poor and poverty are an inescapable and constant presence afflicting every society.

If poverty cannot be eliminated, then the most that can be done is to ameliorate the sufferings of the poor in such a way that they will not feel resentment towards the rich and privileged and be tempted to revolt against them. Revolution, the worst sin imaginable to Donoso, is the complete overthrow of the divinely sanctioned hierarchical order of society. The stability of that order depends upon relieving the plight of the poor through the distribution of alms by the rich and privileged. In this way the poor are pacified and the rich and privileged are justified in their position of superiority and domination. Charity, therefore, is not an act of love whereby the qualities of real concern, good feelings, and communion with others are manifested. It is an interested utilitarian act meant to pacify the potentially unruly masses in such a way that they are kept resigned to their station in life. Since poverty cannot be eliminated, the rich and privileged must be charitable to the poor and the poor must love their patrons and be resigned to their situation. The giving of alms to the poor keeps them "anesthetized" to the reality of the situation that limits their existence. Charity on the part of the rich and privileged and resignation on the part of the poor are essential dispositions necessary for maintaining social order and harmony.

As Paulo Freire points out, the maintenance of an authoritarian and paternalistic social order depends upon fostering the proper attitudes within those who live in that order. This must be done in such a way that they are reconciled and resigned to their situation and cannot envision something different or better for themselves.[121] They are submerged in a one-dimensional social reality they perceive as natural, inescapable, immutable, and inevitable. Life can only be seen by them in one way, especially if they are secure and provided for in any degree.

Life is thus seen as a static phenomenon ever fated to be a "valley of tears" that is endured, not questioned or transcended. To Donoso, poverty is a permanent and necessary feature of life, affording the rich and privileged the opportunity to be charitable in the same way that human misery is essential so that God can be merciful and just. Thus Donoso, like his predecessor de Maistre, presents us with a rhetorically eloquent but dark and pessimistic picture of human life. It is a life weighed down by evil propensities, ignorance, error, inescapable fate, unending misery, violence, and oppression. Nothing can be done to change this state of things. For Donoso, the most that we can do is mitigate the effects of this state of things and be patient and resigned with our lot.

THE WAR OF DOGMA CONTRA DOGMA

Donoso's thought is rooted in a sanctification of dogma. Dogma, for Donoso, is absolutely necessary in order to give guidance to corrupt, irrational, and confused human beings. In this sense, dogma functions in the same way as the totalitarian ideological systems criticized by Václav Havel. What Havel writes about such systems can also be said about Donoso's notion of dogma.

> The more slavishly and dogmatically a person falls for a ready-made ideological system or "worldview," the more certainly he will bury all chances of thinking, of freedom, of being clear about what he knows, the more certainly he will deaden the adventure of the mind and the more certainly—in practice—he will begin to serve the "order of death." In any case, the moment when any system of thought culminates and declares itself complete, when it is brought to perfection and universality, has more than once been described as that deceptive moment when the system ceases to live, collapses in upon itself (like the material collapse of a white dwarf star) and reality eludes its grasp once and for all.[122]

By declaring Catholicism "a complete system of civilization"[123] and the repository of all truth,[124] Donoso embraces a totalitarian ideology based upon and supported by a collection of dogmas. Catholicism, as envisioned by Donoso, is a totalitarian system with an ideology locked in a Manichæan-like life and death struggle with, and seeking to overthrow, other systems armed with their dogmas. Donoso's totalitarian Catholicism is inextricably submerged in a war of "dogma contra dogma."

Donoso's totalitarian notion of Catholicism, which is contained in his dualistic understanding of reality, is locked in a quasi-Manichæan cataclysmic struggle with two other ideological camps—liberalism and socialism—for the control of society. He is neither interested in dialogue nor in open and critical inquiry. The truth in its totality was held by him to reside in Catholicism. There is no truth outside Catholicism. Truth is identical to Catholicism; truth is *Catholic* truth. For Donoso, outside of Catholicism there is only the darkness of error. The truth that is found only within Catholicism can be either accepted or rejected. There can be no neutral or agnostic position between acceptance and rejection for such a position is itself a form of rejection. The rejection of Catholicism is tantamount to the rejection of truth. If truth is rejected, though, it must be dictatorially imposed for the salvific good of all and for the good of political and social order.

Dictatorship is the instrument for the imposition of this dogmatic truth. This dictatorship must be exercised only by those who can claim to possess infallible authority—the Pope of Rome, the Roman clergy, and legitimate temporal rulers. In this way the exercise of dictatorial and infallible authority becomes the instrument that Donoso proposes as the means to impose, save, and maintain civilization. The power that deploys this authority is coterminous with civil society. There can be no civilization without a power that is its unifying principle.[125] Realistically, though, the most that this exercise of authority can accomplish is to help establish and maintain someone in power. For the war of "dogma contra dogma" actually has no relationship with the pursuit of truth, or what Havel calls "living in truth," but with the establishment and maintenance of power. While this may be an effective way to establish and maintain power, at least for a time, it is also an escape from and a denial of reality. Sooner or later such systems of power and control collapse, as we saw in the collapse of the Soviet Union and its totalitarian empire.

Reality has a way of asserting and reasserting itself in the face of lies or of anything that presents itself as being the sole guardian and possessor of the truth because "all constructs of the human mind, whether they are confined to the inner recesses of our thinking or find expression in the outside world in the form of disciplines, ideologies, or institutions, are in some way deficient."[126] The "order of Being," or reality, cannot be suppressed by claims that it is completely understood. Such claims can only spell the end of the "order of Being." It would mean the death of reality, the end of truth in the Havelian sense of striving to live in truth:

> The order of Being has many facets; it can be regarded from many different points of view and experienced on many different levels; it is not within the powers of the "order of the spirit" to grasp it entirely—that is, to reveal its secrets. To do that would require, de facto, an act of absolute merging, and that would mean the end of the "order of the spirit," if not the "order of Being" as well—total death. All one can do . . . is to touch, for better or for worse, a particular level of reality, and apply and develop a particular way of looking at it and experiencing it.[127]

Reality is complex and multidimensional. It is not possible for any one person, group, institution, or ideology to completely understand it. Reality, as part and parcel of the "order of Being," eludes such a grasp. Many see this situation as threatening to themselves and their world. They therefore seek to replace complexity with simplicity, multidimensionality with unidimensionality, questions with absolute answers. As understood by Donoso, this is the rôle of dogma, and of the forms of infallible and dictatorial authority used to impose and maintain it. Dogmatism is an attempt to suppress the very "order of Being." Reality is either made to conform to an ideology or is replaced by it. Every effort must be made to coerce people to accept or acquiesce to this ideologized reality. But when people have to be forced or fooled into believing something, it means that they cannot be convinced through persuasion. The very fact that an ideology must be promoted by coercive or deceptive means attests to its fragility, as well as to the enduring nature of the "order of Being." The "order of Being" can never be confined by or contained in any ideological system. Human life always has a way of resisting such confinement and of eluding dogmatic explanations. As Havel explains it,

> life may be subjected to a prolonged and thorough process of violation, enfeeblement, and anesthesia. Yet, in the end, it cannot be permanently halted. Albeit quietly, covertly, and slowly, it nevertheless goes on. Though it be estranged from itself a thousand times, it always manages in some way to recuperate; however violently ravished, it always survives, in the end, the power which ravished it.[128]

The complex and multidimensional nature of reality also beckons us to view Donoso's notions on human nature with much skepticism. Are human beings really depraved and corrupt in essence? Is there a natural affinity between human reason and absurdity? Is this the most we can say about human nature? If we answer all these question in the affirmative, then it seems we cannot escape concluding that there is an essential futility to human existence. Such futility means that we cannot possibly hope for anything better for ourselves or improve our lot in any way.

Human beings, Donoso holds, are nothing more than irrational and bellicose beasts that need to be kept under strict control lest they destroy themselves and one another. Thus parliamentary liberal democracy cannot work; only dictatorship is feasible as the way to govern the human beast. But if Donoso's picture of human nature is incomplete, then our skepticism is entirely warranted.

The twentieth century alone has supplied us with more than enough examples of human depravity, as we see in the Holocaust and the Soviet Gulag, products of two of the most horrendous dictatorships in human history. In fact, the Nazi and Soviet dictatorships were the main instigators of the most bestial savagery of our age—World War II. Instead of taming the human beast, which is the essential claim of Donoso's theory of dictatorship, these dictatorships unleashed the "beast" and thereby produced a cataclysm of war and genocide. But with the growing concern for human rights since World War II—and with the many positive advances in, for example, medicine and technology—is it also possible to point to something noble, intelligent, and good in human nature? If this is possible, then maybe liberal democratic parliamentarianism might not be a political form unsuitable for human societies.

Juan Donoso Cortés is a key figure in the "war" of "dogma contra dogma" that substitutes ideology for reality, operating under the assumption that dogma is an essential element of social order and stability. The burning question that we are faced with is whether or not we can think about humanity and society, establish institutions, and embrace customs that do not fall into this dogmatic trap. Can we build and maintain societies and institutions upon principles that are neither dogmatic nor dogmatically interpreted? Can we speak of absolutes that are neither dogmatic nor dogmatically conceived? Can we conceive of the absolute without being absolutist?

Given the history of the past two millennia, the prospects for such developments do not seem to be very bright. For some reason we tend to stop short of such a breakthrough. Out of some need for certainty or some Faustian agreement that is made to ease the tensions of existence, human beings continually fall into the absolutist trap. Dark or ignoble tendencies within the human psyche exert in greater or lesser degrees a type of gravitational pull on us in such a way that our nobler tendencies never achieve full sway. However, it is not inevitable that the dark and ignoble tendencies must always attain hegemony over our nobler ones.[129]

Havel observes that noble as well as the ignoble tendencies are present in all people in varying degrees:

> The essential aims of life are present naturally in every person. In everyone there is some longing for humanity's rightful dignity, for moral integrity, for the free expression of being, and a sense of transcendence over the world of existence. Yet, at the same time, each person is capable, to a greater or lesser degree, of coming to terms with living within the lie. Each person somehow succumbs to a profane trivialization of his or her inherent humanity, and to utilitarianism. In everyone there is some willingness to merge with the anonymous crowd and to flow comfortably along with it down the river of pseudo-life.[130]

To the degree that we live "within a lie" we are susceptible to the lure of dogmatism. But, to the degree that we strive to achieve "humanity's rightful dignity," the "free expression of being," and "transcendence," we break free from that lure. But Havel acknowledges here that we never totally break free from it. In greater or lesser degrees this lure, this susceptibility, is woven into the fabric of human life. It is part and parcel of the human condition. It is one of the more prominent features among the many weaknesses that afflict human beings. Yet, the degree in which we are able to understand this constitutes in itself some kind of breakthrough from this lure. We can at least be conscious of the foibles and fragility of our existence and attain a degree of knowledge about its workings. We can also bring about a type of hegemony of the nobler side of these tendencies over the ignoble ones. In an imperfect world perfection is not attainable. However, some modicum of improvement in the human lot is possible. We see this not only in the improved material conditions of life that are spreading throughout the world, but also in the growing universal acceptance of democracy, cultural and social pluralism, and human rights.[131]

This is not possible for an ideological dogmatist like Donoso. He does not even recognize dogmatism as a lure; he does not believe it is possible for our nobler tendencies to achieve a hegemony over our ignoble ones. What Havel understands as a trivialization of life Donoso embraces and holds as essential to it; what Havel sees as an affliction Donoso sees as a cure. Berdyaev views such a situation in terms of the struggle human beings have with the myriad of illusions that can afflict and intrude upon human consciousness:

> Human consciousness is subject to a variety of illusions in understanding the relation between this world in which man feels himself to be in a state of servitude, and the other world in which he awaits his liberation. . . . This world is the world of objectivization, of determinism, of alienation, of hostility, of law. While the other world is the world of spirituality, of freedom, love, kinship.[132]

Donoso belongs to the world of objectivism, determinism, alienation, hostility, and law. His world is one that is senseless and hostile and, therefore, must be controlled through the use of brute force. Meaning must be imposed upon it by means of dogmatic pronouncements and the evil propensities of human beings must be contained through repression. Dictatorship, both political and religious, is the only way to conquer error as well as evil. Dogma and infallible authority are the instruments and the legitimation of that dictatorship. Authority is the insturment and the legitimization of power.

What is ironic about this is that in his dictatorial quest to restore the old modes and orders of what he characterizes as "Catholic civilization," Donoso places himself squarely within the modern world he so despised. There is no breakthrough in Donoso's thought, no transcendence to a higher plane of insight. There is merely the modernistic imposition of power over matter combined with the ideological rationalization of that action. Once we strip away all the trappings of eloquence, logic, and piety we are confronted with someone imprisoned in a quasi-Manichæan power struggle, which is one of the distinguishing characteristics of modernity.

Donoso is just another figure in a war of dogmas. He can be seen as a Jacobin of the right and a "Catholic" Machiavellian seeking to justify a social, political, and religious order that maintains itself through the use of spiritual and physical violence, something akin to the violence of de Maistre and Georges Sorel.[133] What he considers "Catholic" is nothing more than an ideological synthesis of Greco-Roman paganism, Hobbesian anthropology, Calvinism, Machiavellian *Realpolitik*, and romantic medievalism. This is what caused him to miss entirely the significance of modernity as well as the questions that are central to it. This is also at the heart of his philosophical and theological contribution to the tragedies and suffering of our age. Dogmatism—ideological intransigence—has a way of wreaking horror and destruction upon the human family.

Isaiah Berlin remarks:

> What do men do and suffer, and why and how? It is the view that answers to these questions can be provided by formulating general laws, from which the past and future of individuals and societies can be successfully predicted, that has led to misconceptions alike in theory and practice: to fanciful, pseudo-scientific histories and theories of human behaviour, abstract and formal at the expense of the facts, and to revolutions and wars and ideological campaigns conducted on the basis of dogmatic certainty about their outcome—vast misconceptions which have cost the lives, liberty, and happiness of a great many innocent human beings.[134]

The situation in which we find ourselves today can be seen as the very "order of Being" calling upon us[135] to transcend dogmatism in an effort to create a "new world order" wherein dispositions like freedom, creativity, responsibility, reason, faith, community, individuality, love, hope, and loyalty are real and tangible. That such dispositions have a real and tangible content gives testimony to the existence of absolutes. However, they also give testimony to the notion that these absolutes need not be interpreted in a dogmatic or absolutist way. Thus, we cannot explain or define them in any exhaustive way. But we see them as revealing the dimensions of spiritual and moral depth that lie at the heart of reality. In this way we make ourselves open and available to the "order of Being." For it is by making ourselves open and available to that mystery, rather than by a decisionistic imposition of the will upon Every, that leads to life in truth. This is the challenge of our time, a challenge that ideologues of both the left and the right or of any stripe, as well as religious dogmatists (fundamentalists), have failed to grasp. This is why it is so important that we study and understand the ideas of ideological thinkers like Donoso. They provide us with vivid examples of authoritarian and totalitarian thinking while also allowing us to trace the development of ideological trajectories that have been enormously and tragically influential in our times.

A FINAL NOTE

The years 1849–1853 represent the time of Donoso's prominence as a spokesman for the reactionary and authoritarian conservative camp. Along with the *Ensayo*, the works in this volume are among the most important ones from that period and are arranged in chronological order.

I dedicate this work to my teacher, friend, and colleague Frederick G. Lawrence of the Department of Theology at Boston College. It was made possible due to his strong encouragement and support.

NOTES

1. His full name was Juan Francisco María de la Salud Donoso Cortés. He carried the noble titles of Marquis of Valdegamas and Viscount of Valle. On his mother's side he was related to the Spanish conqueror of Mexico, Hernan Cortés. Donoso served as a member of the Spanish Cortes (the Spanish parliament), the Spanish ambassador to Prussia and France, a government minister, and advisor to Queen María Cristina. His speeches and writings were very well-known and influential in Europe in the mid-nineteenth century. See Gabriel de Armas, *Donoso Cortés: su sentido trascendente de la vida* (Madrid: Colección Cálamo, 1953); John T. Graham, *Donoso Cortés: Utopian Romanticist and Political Realist* (Columbia: University of Missouri Press, 1974); R. A. Herrera, *Donoso Cortés: Cassandra of the Age* (Grand Rapids: Eerdmans, 1995); Ramon Menéndez Pidal, *La Historia de España: la era Isabelina y el sexenio democrático (1834–1874)*, vol. XXXIV (Madrid: Espasa Calpe, 1981); Thomas Molnar, *The Counterrevolution* (New York: Funk & Wagnalls, 1969), pp. 4, 142.

The theme concerning generations of revolution and reaction is developed by the Brazilian Catholic and conservative thinker Plinio Corrêa de Oliveira, *Révolution et contre-révolution* (São Paulo: Edições Catolicismo, 1960).

2. See Friedrich Heer, *Europe, Mother of Revolutions*, trans. Charles Kessler and Jennetta Adcock (London: Weidenfield and Nicolson, 1971), pp. 7–12, 251–253; see also Molnar, ibid., pp. 4, 23, 34–35, 66–68, 91–92, 104, 107–109, 112, 113, 142, 194–195.

3. See Joseph de Maistre, *Du Pape dans son rapport avec les souverainetés temporelles* (Paris: Librairie Catholique Emmanuel Vitte, 1928), Chaps. 8–10; Hans Küng, *On Being a Christian*, trans. Edward Quinn (Garden City: Doubleday, Image, 1976), p. 556.

4. See Carl Schmitt, *The Concept of the Political*, trans. George Schwab (Chicago: University of Chicago Press, 1996), pp. 61, 65, 70; idem, *Political Theology*, trans. George Schwab (Cambridge: MIT Press, 1985), pp. 37, 51–66.

5. See Schmitt, *The Concept of the Political*, pp. 26–58; Juan Donoso Cortés, *Letter to the Editors of* El Pais *and* El Heraldo; idem, *Letters to the Count of Montalembert.* See also Wolfgang Palaver, *Die mythischen Quellen des Politischen: Carl Schmitts Freund-Feind-Theorie* (Stuttgart: Kohlhammer, 1998), pp. 20–21.

6. See Stephen Holmes, *The Anatomy of Antiliberalism* (Cambridge: Harvard

University Press, 1993), pp. 13–60.

7. See Carl Schmitt, *Donoso Cortés in gesamteuropäische Interpretation* (Cologne: Greven, 1950); in Spanish, *La interpretación europea de Donoso Cortés* (Madrid: Rialp, 1953).

8. See Schmitt, *Political Theology*, pp. 53–66.

9. See John P. McCormick, *Carl Schmitt's Critique of Liberalism: Against Politics as Technology* (Cambridge: University of Cambridge Press, 1997).

10. See "Law on the Principles of the National Movement," 17 May 1958, Article II, in *The Spanish Constitution: Fundamental Laws of the State* (Madrid: SIE, 1972), p. 43. Ibid., p. 49: "Statute Law of the Spanish People," 17 July 1945, Article VI. Ibid., p. 109: "Law of Succession in the Headship of State," 26 July 1947, Article I; Raymond Carr, *Spain: 1808–1975* (Oxford: Clarendon, 1982), p. 763; Alistair Hennesy, "Fascism and Populism in Latin America" in Walter Laqueur, editor, *Fascism: A Reader's Guide* (Berkeley: University of California Press, 1976), p. 256.

11. While it may be more accurate to describe these régimes as conservative authoritarian, they can also be referred to as semi-fascist since they incorporated certain trappings and ideological elements of fascism. See Stanley Payne, *Fascism: Comparison and Definition* (Madison: University of Wisconsin Press, 1980), p. 15–18; idem, *A History of Fascism: 1914–1945* (Madison: University of Wisconsin Press, 1995), pp. 16–19. See also Martin Blinkhorn, "Introduction: Allies, Rival, or Antagonists? Fascists and Conservatives in Modern Europe" in Martin Blinkhorn, editor, *Fascists and Conservatives* (London: Unwin Hyman, 1990), pp. 1–13; Zeev Sternhell, *Neither Right nor Left: Fascist Ideology in France* (Princeton: Princeton University Press, 1986), p. xvii.

12. See Tom Buchanan and Martin Conway, editors, *Political Catholicism in Europe, 1918–1965* (Oxford: Clarendon Press, 1996), pp. 7, 54–57, 136–149; also Payne, *A History of Fascism*, pp. 248–249, 313, 397–398; Philippe Pétain, *Actes et ecrits*, editor Jacques Isorni (Paris: Flammarion, 1974), pp. 478–481, 529–531; Francisco Franco, "Speech to the Extraordinary Session of the Spanish Cortes," 22 November 1966 in *The Spanish Constitution: The Fundamental Laws of the State*, pp. 19–37.

13. Louis Veuillot (1813–1883), editor of the Ultramontanist and conservative Catholic publication *L'Univers*, a close friend of Donoso, and a chief spokesman for conservatism and Ultramontanism in France in the nineteenth century. Ultramontanists were supporters of a strong, authoritarian, and centralized papacy with the Church and civil society under its firm dominion. The term "Ultramontane" comes from the French "*outre montagnes*," that is, "on the other side of the mountains." The mountains in question were the Alps. The pope resided on the other side of the Alps. To be an Ultramontanist meant to be loyal to the one who resides on the other side of the mountains—the pope. Louis Veuillot was the principal leader and spokesman for the Ultramontanist movement in France during the nineteenth century. On Ultramontanism see John C. Rao, "Louis Veuillot and Catholic 'Intransigence': A Re-evaluation," *Faith and Reason* IX, 4 (Winter 1983), pp. 282–306; Thomas Bokenkotter, *A Concise History of the Catholic Church* (Garden City: Doubleday, Image, 1979), p. 312; Fernand Mourret, *A History of the Catholic Church*, vol. 8, trans. Newton Thompson (St. Louis: Herder, 1957).

14. See Friedrich Heer, *Europe: Mother of Revolutions* (London: Weidenfield and Nicolson, 1971), p. 259; Payne, *A History of Fascism*, pp. 41–42; Roger Grif-

fin, *The Nature of Fascism* (New York: Routledge, 1993), pp. 50–51, 212–215; Juan J. Linz, "Some Notes Toward a Comparative Study of Fascism in Sociological Historical Perspective" in Walter Laqueur, editor, *Fascism: A Readers Guide* (Berkeley: University of California Press, 1976), p. 9.

15. See Graham, *Donoso Cortés*, p. 193.

16. De Maistre has a particularly macabre view of humans. However, as a brilliant stylist, he expresses that view with a peculiar eloquence when he writes:

> evil has stained everything *and man in his entirety is nothing but a malady.* An incredible combination of two different and incompatible powers, a monstrous centaur, he feels that he is the result of some unknown crime, some detestable mixture that has corrupted him even in his deepest nature.

Joseph de Maistre, *The Saint Petersburg Dialogues* in *The Works of Joseph de Maistre*, trans. and editor Jack Lively (New York: Schocken, 1971), p. 199.

17. Czeslaw Milosz, *The Captive Mind*, trans. Jane Zielonko (New York: Vintage, 1953), p. 77; see also Eric Hoffer, *The True Believer* (New York: HarperCollins, 1951), pp. 105–111.

18. Albert Camus, *The Myth of Sisyphus and Other Essays*, trans. Justin O'Brien (New York: Vintage, 1955), p. 5.

19. Ibid., pp. 21–48.

20. Nicolai Berdyaev, *Slavery and Freedom*, trans. R. M. French (New York: Scribners, 1944), p. 139.

21. See Niccolò Machiavelli, *The Prince*, trans. Harvey C. Mansfield, Jr. (Chicago: University of Chicago Press, 1985), Chap. 17.

22. See Plato, *Republic*, 414c–415c; de Maistre, *Study on Sovereignty* in *Works*, pp. 108–109.

23. See Gabriel de Armas, "Donoso Cortés, maximo apologista y el *Syllabus*," *El Español* (7 December 1946); Yves Chiron, *Pie IX: pape moderne* (Condé-sur-Noireau: Clovis, 1995); Graham, *Donoso Cortés*, pp. 267, 295–296; Luis Ortiz Estrada, "Donoso Cortés, Veuillot y el *Syllabus* de Pio IX," *Reconquista* 1 (1950), pp. 15–37; Raúl Sánchez Abelenda, *La teoría del poder en el pensamiento político de Juan Donoso Cortés* (Buenos Aires: Editorial Universitaria de Buenos Aires, 1969), p. 98.

24. Reasonableness, attentiveness, intelligence, and responsibility are described by Bernard Lonergan as "transcendental precepts" that constitute the substance of the notion of authenticity. See Bernard Lonergan, *A Third Collection*, editor Frederick Crowe (New York: Paulist Press, 1985), p. 7; see also Charles Taylor, *The Ethics of Authenticity* (Cambridge: Harvard University Press, 1991), pp. 27–28, 39, 67–69.

25. Joseph de Maistre, *Du Pape dans son rapport avec l'Eglise catholique*, Bk. I, Chap. 1.

26. See Graham, *Donoso Cortés*, pp. 267, 294, 297.

27. See ibid., p. 297; Bokenkotter, *A Concise History of the Catholic Church*, pp. 318–339; idem, *Essential Catholicism: Dynamics of Faith and Belief* (New York: Doubleday, Image, 1986), p. 121; Hans Küng, *Infallibility?: An Inquiry*, trans. Edward Quinn (Garden City: Doubleday, 1971), pp. 89–94.

28. "Fortified by the acts of the First Vatican Council, Pius [IX] continued his policy of intransigence toward modern secular liberal culture and showed clearly that he was unable to adapt the Church to the profound social and political transformations going on around him. At his death in 1878 the Church was left in a virtual state

of war with the rest of society—a *Kulturkampf* by no means limited to Bismarck's Germany." Bokenkotter, *A Concise History of the Catholic Church*, p. 338. On the efforts of Catholics to reconcile the Church with the contemporary world see Thomas Bokenkotter, *Church and Revolution: Catholics in the Struggle for Democracy and Social Justice* (New York: Doubleday, 1998).

29. Gary Lease, *"Odd Fellows" in the Politics of Religion: Modernism, National Socialism, and German Judaism* (New York: Mouton de Gruyter, 1995), p. 55; see also Bokenkotter, ibid., pp. 317–339, 407–408.

30. See Lease, ibid., pp. 21–133; idem, "Vatican Foreign Policy and the Origins of Modernism," paper delivered at the Seminar on Roman Catholic Modernism at the annual meeting of the American Academy of Religion, New Orleans, November 1996; also Bokenkotter, ibid., pp. 356–367; Heer, *Europe: Mother of Revolutions*, pp. 283–300.

31. Edgar J. Jung, "Germany and the Conservative Revolution" in Anton Kaes, Martin Jay, and Edward Dimendberg, editors, *The Weimar Republic Sourcebook* (Berkeley: University of California Press, 1994), p. 352. See also Klaus Fritzsche, *Politische Romantik und Gegenrevolution: Fluchtwege in der Krise der bürgerlichen Gesellschaft–Das Beispiel des "Tat" Kreises* (Frankfurt: Suhrkamp, 1976); Jeffrey Herf, *Reactionary Modernism: Technology, Culture, and Politics in Weimar and the Third Reich* (New York: Cambridge University Press, 1984); Armin Mohler, *Die Konservative Revolution in Deutschland: 1918–1932* (Darmstadt: Wissenschaftliche Buchgesellschaft, 1972); Otto-Ernst Schüddekopf, *Linke Leute von Rechts: Nationalbolschewismus in Deutschland 1918–1933* (Frankfurt: Ullstein, 1972); Kurt Sontheimer, *Antidemokratisches Denken in Deutschland: 1918–1932* (Munich: Nymphenburger Verlagshandlung, 1968); Fritz Richard Stern, *The Politics of Cultural Despair: A Study in the Rise of Germanic Ideology* (Garden City: Anchor, 1965).

32. See Blinkhorn, "Introduction: Allies, Rivals, or Antagonists?" in *Fascists and Conservatives*, pp. 1–13; Payne, *A History of Fascism*, p. 162; Mark Neocleous, *Fascism* (Minneapolis: University of Minnesota Press, 1997), pp. 69–74; José Antonio Primo de Rivera, *Obras de José Antonio Primo de Rivera*, 8th edition, editor Agustín del Rio Cisneros (Madrid: Delegación de la Sección Femenina del Movimiento, 1974), pp. 85–93.

33. Joseph Bendersky, *Carl Schmitt: Theorist for the Reich* (Princeton: Princeton University Press, 1983), pp. 56–57. See also Griffin, *The Nature of Fascism*, p. 91.

34. Some connect Schmitt with the conservative revolution and the effort to undermine the Weimar Republic. According to Joseph Bendersky and George Schwab, even though Schmitt had reservations about the Weimar Republic and "certain affinities" with the conservative revolutionaries, he never associated with their movement. His theories on dictatorship are in the context of his writings on Article 48 of the Weimar Constitution wherein he advocates a strong presidency, with dictatorial powers to be used in exceptional circumstances, within the republican political framework. However, Schmitt's authoritarian conservative views, especially his ideas on the need for the masses to be directed and governed by an élite, made it possible for him to support the National Socialists after Hitler came to power. Schmitt joined the Nazi party in 1933 and was connected to the Nazi régime in its early years. See Bendersky, ibid., pp. 56–61, 195–218; idem, "Carl Schmitt and the Conservative Revolution," *Telos* 72 (Summer 1987); Renato Cristi, *Carl Schmitt and Authoritarian Liber-*

alism: Strong State, Free Economy (Cardiff: University of Wales Press, 1998); George Schwab, *The Challenge of the Exception: An Introduction to the Political Ideas of Carl Schmitt between 1921 and 1936*, 2nd ed., (Westport: Greenwood, 1989), pp. 37–43, 101–143; idem, "Introduction" in Schmitt, *Political Theology*, pp. xiii–xiv. See also Gordon A. Craig, *Germany: 1866–1945* (Oxford: Oxford University Press, 1980), p. 494; Roger Eatwell, *Fascism: A History* (New York: Penguin, 1995), pp. 150, 288, 314, 350; Holmes, *The Anatomy of Antiliberalism*, pp. 37–60; McCormick, *Carl Schmitt's Critique of Liberalism*, pp. 11–15, 298–299; George L. Mosse, *The Crisis of German Ideology: Intellectual Origins of the Third Reich* (New York: Grosset & Dunlap, 1964), pp. 283–285; Tracy B. Strong, "Forward: Dimensions of the New Debate Around Carl Schmitt" in Schmitt, *The Concept of the Political*, pp. ix–xiii.

35. Mark Neocleous writes that "we can describe fascism as the culmination of the *conservative revolutionary* tradition." Neocleous, ibid., p. 57; see also F. L. Carsten, *The Rise of Fascism* (London: Methuen, 1967), pp. 9–44; Griffin, ibid., pp. 91–92; Linz, "Some Notes Toward a Comparative Study of Fascism in Sociological Historical Perspective" in Laqueur, *Fascism*, pp. 26–28, 30–32; Payne, *A History of Fascism*, pp. 37–41; Robert Soucy, *French Fascism: The Second Wave, 1933–1939* (New Haven: Yale University Press, 1995), pp. 6, 20, 27, 252, 308, 310, 317; H. R. Trevor-Roper, "The Phenomenon of Fascism" in S. J. Woolf , editor, *European Fascism* (New York: Vintage, 1969), pp. 18–38.

36. Donoso was influenced by the cyclical theories of history of Vico and Hegel. With de Maistre he shared an apocalyptic view of history wherein God acts through human events like wars and revolutions. Along with Plato, Aristotle, Augustine, and Aquinas, Donoso shared the belief in certain metaphysical presuppositional *absolutes* or *norms* that stand above all human action and to which that action must conform. His view of human nature reflects the dark and pessimistic view of it as corrupt and depraved that is found in the writings of Augustine, Machiavelli, Hobbes, Calvin, and de Maistre.

37. Pierre-Joseph Proudhon (1809–1865), prominent and influential early French socialist, regarded as a prominent philosopher of anarchism. His ideas first appeared in 1840 in his book *What Is Property?* in which he views the personal ownership of property as a grave social evil. He is Donoso's *bête noire*.

Donoso's reaction against Proudhon was based upon a misunderstanding and a distortion of Proudhon's position, according to Friedrich Heer:

> His [Proudhon's] premise, "God is evil," was based on an argument that the traditional interpretation of the Godhead placed men squarely in their state of misery and left no room for progress. History was not a series of operatic scenes wherein God and the Devil fought one another, but a process of antagonistic principles. The Devil was freedom and decisively rejected the kings, priests, and law-givers of the old world. This freedom, so wrongly called devilish, was the major force behind creative energy. "Freedom, to you, is Anti-Christ, the Devil," Proudhon wrote to the Archbishop of Besançon.

Proudhon, who had nothing but contempt for Donoso, easily could have written this to Donoso, whom he saw as "a pharasaical Jesuit and fanatical Spanish inquisitor." Donoso's inability or unwillingness to distinguish hyperbolic expression from philosophical substance enabled him to distort Proudhon's position. By misrepresenting him, Donoso created a straw man for himself. Without the straw man, Donoso's polemic rings hollow. But the creation of a straw man may also be a sign of the sort of paranoia and hysteria that usually reigns in times of social tension and revolutionary change. (Heer, *Europe: Mother of Revolutions*, p. 98. See also Juan Donoso Cortés, *Ensayo sobre el catolicismo, el liberalismo y el socialismo*, Bk. I, Chap. 1; Graham, *Donoso Cortés*, p. 287.)

38. Carl Schmitt denies the idea that Donoso's stance after 1848 was a result of panic. He observes that before the terrible events of 1848, Donoso was already a conservative. But rather than disprove the notion that Donoso's post-1848 stance was a result of panic, the idea that he was already a conservative reinforces this notion. Donoso's conservatism, which rests upon a firm belief in order and authority, can be seen as something that ideologically disposed him to panic in the face of revolutionary change, as we see in his frantic advocacy of dictatorship in order to stop the revolutionary tide. Schmitt, however, tries to dismiss the charge of panic as a sort of *ex post facto* psychological and sociological analysis. But he fails to demonstrate how or why such an analysis is useless. He ridicules the notion of panic, but he offers no coherent argument against it. (See Schmitt, *La interpretación europea de Donoso Cortés*, pp. 32–33.) Václav Havel discusses the reactionary nature of panic in his open letter to Gustav Husak, former president of Czechoslovakia, "Dear Dr. Husak" in *Open Letters*, ed. Paul Wilson (New York: Knopf, 1991), p. 76.

39. Donoso Cortés, *Ensayo*, Bk. I, Chap. 2.

40. Paulo Freire, *Education for Critical Consciousness*, trans. Myra Bergman Ramos (New York: Continuum, 1994), pp. 21–24.

41. Isaiah Berlin, *The Crooked Timber of Humanity*, editor Henry Hardy (New York: Vintage, 1990), pp. 93–94.

42. Ibid., p. 96.

43. Ibid., pp. 91–174.

44. See Erich Fromm, *Man for Himself* (New York: Henry Holt, 1947), pp. 8–14.

45. See Zeev Sternhell, "The Crisis of *fin-de-siècle* Thought" in Roger Griffin, editor, *International Fascism: Theories, Causes and the New Consensus* (London: Oxford University Press, 1998), pp. 169–174.

46. Griffin, *The Nature of Fascism*, p. 202.

47. See ibid., pp. 202–205.

48. See Jules Chaix-Ruy, *Donoso Cortés: Théologien de l'histoire et prophète* (Paris: Beauchesne, 1956); Graham, *Donoso Cortés*, p. 141; Herrera, *Donoso Cortés: Cassandra of the Age*, pp. 116–135; idem, "Donoso Cortés: A Second Look at Political Apocalyptic," *Continuity*, 11 (1987); Bela Menczer, "A Prophet of Europe's Disasters," *The Month*, 183 (May 1947). See also Molnar, *The Counter-Revolution*, p. 122.

49. See Charles Maurras, *Mes idées politiques* (Paris: Fayard, 1937); Primo de Rivera, *Obras*; T. S. Eliot, *The Idea of a Christian Society* (New York: Harcourt, Brace and Company, 1940) and *Notes Toward a Definition of Culture* (London: Faber and Faber, 1948); Henri Massis, *Defense of the West*, trans. F. S. Flint (New York: Harcourt, Brace, and Company, 1928); Benito Mussolini, "The Doctrine of Fascism," trans. Jane Soames, *Social and Political Philosophy*, editors John Somerville and Ronald E. Santoni (New York: Doubleday, 1963), pp. 424–440; Ramiro de Maeztu, *Defensa del espiritu* (Madrid: Ediciones Rialp, 1958); idem, *Ensayos*, (Buenos Aires: Emecé Editores, 1948); idem, *El nuevo tradicionalismo y la revolución social*, (Madrid: Editora Nacional, 1959). On Gentile, D'Annunzio, de Benoist, Jünger, and Schmitt see Roger Griffin, editor, *Fascism* (New York: Oxford University Press,

1995), pp. 35–37, 53–54, 108–109, 111–112, 138–139, 346–348. On Peguy see David Carroll, *French Literary Fascism* (Princeton: Princeton University Press, 1995), pp. 42–70. See also Martin Blinkhorn, "The Iberian States" in Detlef Mühlberger, editor, *The Social Basis of European Fascist Movements* (London: Croom Helm, 1987), pp. 320–348; Sternhell, ibid.

50. This opposition to liberalism is problematic to Leo Strauss in the case of Carl Schmitt. He claims that Schmitt's "critique of liberalism occurs in the horizon of liberalism; his unliberal tendency is restrained by the still unvanquished 'systematics of liberal thought.'" This is primarily due to the Hobbesian influences in Schmitt's thought. Mark Neocleous sees conservatism in its "counterrevolutionary" aspects as "modernist." Given this understanding of the matter, the antiliberalism of the fascists Mussolini and Primo de Rivera is also within the liberal horizon. In the case of Primo de Rivera we see the influence of the Spanish liberal thinker José Ortega y Gasset. See Leo Strauss, "Notes on Carl Schmitt: *The Concept of the Political*" in Schmitt, *The Concept of the Political*, pp. 106–107; Neocleous, ibid., p. 73; Mussolini, "The Doctrine of Fascism," pp. 434–436; Primo de Rivera, *Obras*, pp. 745–749.

51. See Payne, *A History of Fascism*, pp. 16–19, 277–289, 490.

52. See Primo de Rivera, *Obras*, pp. 92, 343–344, 397.

53. Neocleous, ibid., p. 74.

54. See Donoso Cortés, *Ensayo*, Bk. I, Chap. 6 and Bk. II, Chap. 1; Schmitt, *The Concept of the Political*, p. 61.

55. See Renato Cristi, "Schmitt on Sovereignty and Constituent Power" in David Dyzenhaus, editor, *Law as Politics: Carl Schmitt's Critique of Liberalism* (Durham: Duke University Press, 1998), pp. 182–183; Schwab, *The Challenge of the* Exception, pp. 20–23.

56. Schmitt developed his theories on the exception and dictatorship in his discussions on Article 48 of the Weimar constitution. See Ernst-Wolfgang Böckenförde, "The Concept of the Political: A Key to Understanding Carl Schmitt's Constitutional Theory" in Dyzenhaus, ibid., pp. 41–42; Schwab, *The Challenge of the Exception*, pp. 37–43; idem, "Introduction" in Schmitt, ibid., pp. xix–xxiii.

57. See Schmitt, *Political Theology*, pp. 51–52, 63-66; idem, *The Crisis of Parliamentary Democracy*, trans. Ellen Kennedy (Cambridge: MIT Press, 1985), pp. 48–50; Donoso Cortés, *Speech on Dictatorship*.

58. Holmes, *The Anatomy of Antiliberalism*, p. 19.

59. Gary Lease, "Vatican Foreign Policy," paper for the Seminar on Roman Catholic Modernism, delivered at the annual meeting of the American Academy of Religion, New Orleans, Louisiana, November, 1996.

60. See Donoso Cortés, *Speech on Dictatorship*; see also Sánchez Abelenda, *La teoría del poder*, p. 356.

61. See Donoso Cortés, *Letter to Queen María Cristina*.

62. See Schmitt, *Political Theology*, pp. 51–52, 65–66.

63. Donoso Cortés, *Speech on Dictatorship*.

64. See Lease, *"Odd Fellows,"* p. 159.

65. See Donoso Cortés, ibid.

66. Schmitt, *Political Theology*, p. 36.

67. See Donoso Cortés, *Letters to the Count of Montalembert*.

68. De Maistre, *The Saint Petersburg Dialogues* in *The Works of Joseph de*

Maistre, edited and trans. by Jack Lively (New York: Schocken, 1971), p. 263.

69. See Donoso Cortés, *Ensayo*, Bk. II, Chap. 2; idem, *Speech on Dictatorship.*

70. See Sigmund Freud, *Civilization and Its Discontents*, trans. James Strachey (New York: Norton, 1961), pp. 49–52; Donoso Cortés, *Ensayo*, Bk. I, Chap. 5; idem, *Speech on Dictatorship*. See also Eatwell, *Fascism*, p. 9; Thomas Hobbes, *Leviathan*, editor Edwin Curley (Indianapolis: Hackett, 1994), Chap. XIII; 9, 11–13.

71. Their views differ on how it is useful. Donoso regards religion as an essential and fundamental element for society, while Freud views it as a useful consolation for many insecure and infantile people in a society. See Sigmund Freud, *The Future of an Illusion*, trans. W. D. Robson-Scott (Garden City: Doubleday, 1961), pp. 55–57; Donoso Cortés, *Ensayo*, Bk. I, Chap. 2.

72. See McCormick, *Carl Schmitt's Critique of Liberalism*, pp. 121–127.

73. On the distinction between "commissarial" and "sovereign" dictatorships see Carl Schmitt, *Die Diktatur: Von den Anfängen des modernen Souveränitätsgedankens bis zum proletarischen Klassenkampf* (Berlin: Duncker & Humblot, 1989), pp. xiii, 3, 136, 139–140, 146, 201–202; McCormick, *Carl Schmitt's Critique of Liberalism*, pp. 122–141; Schwab, *The Challenge of the Exception*, pp. 30–37.

74. See McCormick, ibid., pp. 129–132.

75. See Donoso Cortés, *Ensayo*, Bk. III, Chap. 4.

76. See McCormick, *Carl Schmitt's Critique of Liberalism*, p. 132.

77. See Donoso Cortés, *Speech on Dictatorship.*

78. Schmitt, *Political Theology*, pp. 51–52.

79. See Machiavelli, *The Prince*, Chaps. 15 and 25.

80. Donoso Cortés, *Ensayo*, Bk. I, Chap. 2. This understanding of authority is also reflected in the concept of *Jefetura* developed by the Spanish fascist thinker José Antonio Primo de Rivera. See Primo de Rivera, *Obras*, pp. 662–663; see also Francisco Martinell Gifre, *La política con alas: José Antonio, Ramiro y Onésimo desde una perspectiva actual* (Madrid: Ediciones del Movimiento, 1974), pp. 177–183.

81. See Berdyaev, *Slavery and Freedom*, pp. 104–105.

82. Ibid., p. 105.

83. Ibid.

84. On fascist organicism see Primo de Rivera, ibid., pp. 66, 89, 340, 563, 712, 797, 875; see also Mussolini, "Doctrine of Fascism," p. 437.

85. Charles–Forbes Count of Montalembert (1810–1870) was a prominent liberal Catholic in France, supporter of the 1848 revolution, as well as an early supporter of the régime of Napoleon III. He was a friend of Donoso. Montalembert was also the founder of the first Catholic political party in Europe, a partisan for the separation of church and state in France, and a strong opponent of the Ultramontanists and their chief leader, Louis Veuillot. He was critical of the doctrine of papal infallibility, but relented in his criticism after being reprimanded by the papal Curia.

86. Manichæism is based on the teachings of the prophet Mani (third century C.E.). His teachings state that there are "two primary elements, God and Matter," that dominate the cosmos. These elements, according to Geo Widengren, can also be called "Light and Darkness or Truth and Lie. Thus the impersonal concepts of Truth and Light could be regarded as a personal being, God, whilst correspondingly Light and Darkness received not only the impersonal appellation Matter but could also be personified as the 'Prince of Darkness.' This does not, however, mean that the Manichees recognized the existence of two gods." It does, though, denote a dualism

wherein two opposing forces, Good and Evil, are locked in incessant combat. Geo Widengren, *Mani and Manichæism*, trans. Charles Kessler (New York: Holt, Rinehart and Winston, 1965), pp. 43–44. See also Eric Voegelin, *Order and History: The Ecumenic Age*, Volume 4 (Baton Rouge: Louisiana State University Press, 1974), pp. 138–142.

87. Donoso Cortés, *Ensayo*, Bk. II, Chap. 3.

88. "Nothing is plainer to man than the existence of two opposed forces which ceaselessly battle in the universe. There is no good that evil does not defile and debase; there is no evil that good does not restrain and attack, in impelling all things toward a more perfect state. These two forces are everywhere present." De Maistre, *The Generative Principle of Political Constitutions* in *Works*, p. 166.

89. Donoso Cortés, *Ensayo*, Bk. II, Chap. 4.

90. Ibid.

91. See ibid.

92. See ibid.

93. Augustine, *The Enchiridion on Faith, Hope, and Love*, trans. J. F. Shaw (Chicago: Regnery, 1961), XI.

94. Thomas Aquinas, *Compendium theologiæ*, trans. Ross J. Dunn (Toronto: Saint Michael's College, 1934), CXVII. See also idem, *Exposition of the 'De divinis nominibus*,' Part IV, Lecture 14: "Now we can begin to recognize what evil is: it is not a real substance, for evil things are good by their substance, but a deficiency of some good which a thing should possess, but does not."

95. Donoso Cortés, *Ensayo*, Bk. II, Chap. 4.

96. Ibid.

97. Ibid.

98. See ibid., Bk. III, Chap. 2.

99. Aquinas, *Compendium theologiæ*, CXLII.

100. Donoso Cortés, *Ensayo*, Bk. II, Chap. 7.

101. Ibid., Bk. II, Chap. 3; see idem, *Letters to the Count of Montalembert.*

102. Idem, *Ensayo*, Bk. II, Chap. 3.

103. See Donoso Cortés, *Letters to the Count of Montalembert.*

104. See ibid.

105. See Augustine, *City of God*, trans. Gerald G. Walsh, Demetrius B. Zemo, S. J., Grace Monahan, O. S. U., and Daniel J. Honan, editor Vernon J. Bourke (Garden City: Image, 1958), Bk. XV, Chap. 1.

106. Ibid., Bk. XIV, Chap. 1.

107. See Henri de Lubac, *Theological Fragments*, trans. Rebecca Howell Balinski (San Francisco: Ignatius Press, 1989), pp. 235–286.

108. Ibid., pp. 250–251.

109. See Hobbes, *Leviathan*, Chap. 20.

Paul Johnson, *A History of Christianity* (New York: Atheneum, 1976), p. 112.

111. Ibid., pp. 116–117.

112. Donoso Cortés, *Ensayo*, Bk. I, Chap. 3.

113. Carl Schmitt delineates the two civilizations in this manner:

Freedom, progress and reason}	against	{feudalism, reaction and force
in alliance with		in alliance with
economy, industry and technology}	against	{state, war and politics
as		as

parliamentarianism against dictatorship.

(Schmitt, *The Concept of the Political*, p. 75.)

114. Louis de Bonald, *Théorie du pouvoir politique et religieux* (Paris: Union Génerale d'Editions, 1966), p. 105.

115. See Donoso Cortés, *Letters to the Count of Montalembert.*

116. Schmitt, *The Concept of the Political*, p. 35.

117. See Donoso Cortés, *Ensayo*, Bk. I, Chaps. 2 and 3.

118. See Schmitt, *The Crisis of Parliamentary Democracy*, pp. 3, 6–8, 46–49.

119. See Donoso Cortés, *Ensayo*, Bk. III, Chap. 2.

120. See Herbert Marcuse, *One-Dimensional Man* (Boston: Beacon Press, 1964), pp. xvii, 84–120.

121. See Paulo Freire, *Pedagogy of the Oppressed*, trans. Myra Bergman Ramos (New York: Continuum, 1994), pp. 128–133; Marcuse, ibid., pp. 84–120.

122. Václav Havel, *Letters to Olga*, trans. Paul Wilson (New York: Henry Holt, 1989), pp. 191–192.

123. Donoso Cortés, *Ensayo*, Bk. I, Chap. 2.

124. See ibid., Bk. I, Chap. 3.

125. See Sánchez Abelenda, *La teoría del poder*, pp. 357–370; Frederick D. Wilhelmsen, *Christianity and Political Philosophy* (Athens: University of Georgia Press, 1978), pp. 139–173.

126. George Soros, *The Crisis of Global Capitalism: Open Society Endangered* (New York: Public Affairs, 1998), p. 19.

127. Havel, *Letters to Olga*, pp. 190–191.

128. Havel, *Open Letters*, trans. and editor Paul Wilson (New York: Knopf, 1991), p. 75.

129. See Fromm, *Man for Himself*, pp. 226.

130. Václav Havel, "The Power of the Powerless," trans. Paul Wilson, in *Living in Truth*, editor Jan Vladislav (Boston: Faber and Faber, 1986), p. 54.

131. See Francis Fukuyama, *The End of History and the Last Man* (New York: Avon, 1992), pp. 49–50.

132. Berdyaev, *Slavery and Freedom*, p. 254.

133. See de Maistre, *Enlightenment on Sacrifices* in *Works*, pp. 291–298; see also René Girard, *Violence and the Sacred*, trans. Patrick Gregory (Baltimore: Johns Hopkins University Press, 1977), pp. 2, 4, 10; See Georges Sorel, *Reflections on Violence*, trans. T. E. Hulme (London: George Allan & Unwin, 1915; see also Schmitt, *The Crisis of Parliamentary Democracy*, pp. 69–70.

134. Isaiah Berlin, *The Sense of Reality*, editor Henry Hardy (New York: Farrar, Straus and Giroux, 1996), p. 39.

135. Václav Havel writes, "While 'Being'—as the absolute horizon of our relating—is for us—as a 'voice' and a 'cry'—identical with the moral order (as though Being were not only the 'reasoning mind' of everything that exists, but its heart as well), the world, or rather existence in it, is a temptation for us to cling in a more complacent fashion (because of indifference to the difficult 'voice of Being') to superficialities, immediate aims, details, to adapt ourselves to the plow of phenomena while giving up on their meaning (leading inevitably to the weakening on one's own Being)." Havel, *Letters to Olga*, p. 374.

Speech on Dictatorship

Gentlemen,

The long speech delivered yesterday by Mr. Cortina,[1] to which I shall reply in a limited way,[2] was nothing more than a summary, in spite of its enormity. It was a summary of the errors of the Progressive Party, which is nothing more than another summary. This is the summary of all the errors that have been invented within the last three centuries that today more or less disturb every human society.

At the beginning of his speech, Mr. Cortina showed the good faith of a distinguished gentleman. And he displayed so much talent that at times he almost seemed to suspect that his principles would be false and his ideas disastrous when he saw that they would never be in power, but always in opposition. I shall tell the distinguished gentleman that with only a little reflection his doubt could change itself into certitude. His ideas are not in power but are in opposition, precisely because they are ideas of opposition, not of governance. Gentlemen, they are infertile, sterile, and disastrous ideas. It is necessary to combat them until they have been buried here in their natural cemetery, under this vault at the foot of this rostrum.

Mr. Cortina, following the traditions of the party he heads and represents, following, I say, the tradition of this party since the February revolution, delivered a speech divided into three parts. I consider this division inevitable. The first part was an eulogy to the progressive party recounting its past merits. The second part recalled its present grievances. The third part contained a program or an account of its future merits.

Gentlemen of the majority,[3] I shall now defend your principles. However, do not expect a single eulogy from me. You are the victors. And nothing feels so good to the victor as a crown of modesty.

Furthermore, gentlemen, do not expect me to speak about your grievances. You do not have personal grievances to avenge, except for those offenses against society and the Throne committed by traitors to your queen and Fatherland. I also will not speak about your merits. What purpose would that serve? Because the nation is not familiar with them? The nation is indeed very familiar with them.

Mr. Cortina divided his speech into two main parts, the gentlemen deputies may recall. The honorable gentleman dealt with the foreign policy of the government and stated that the events that have taken place in Paris, London, and Rome are of great importance to Spain. I shall also address these matters.

Then the gentleman spoke about domestic policy. According to Mr. Cortina, domestic policy can be divided into two parts—into principles and facts or methods and conduct. Through the Minister of Foreign Affairs and the Minister of the Interior, who discharged their tasks with their usual eloquence, the Cabinet responded to the questions concerning facts and conduct in a fitting manner, considering that they have all the facts. It remains for me to deal with the principles. If the Congress will permit me, I will only undertake this matter.

Gentlemen, what is Mr. Cortina's fundamental point? If I have well analyzed his speech, the fundamental point for the gentleman is the following: it is legality in domestic policy. Everything exists by the exact letter of the law. The law must be exactly followed in all circumstances and on all occasions. Gentlemen, I believe that laws are made for societies, not societies for laws. I say: society, everything through society, everything for society; always society, society in all circumstances and on all occasions.

When the letter of the law is enough to save a society, then the letter of the law is best. But when it is not enough, then dictatorship is best. Gentlemen, this fearful word (and it is fearful, but not as much as the word revolution, the most fearful word of all), this fearful word has been uttered by a man well known to all. This man is certainly the material out of which dictators are made. I naturally understand dictators, but not in order to imitate them. Two things are impossible for me: to condemn dictatorship and to exercise it. Due to this (which I fittingly, nobly, and frankly declare), I am incapable of governing. I could not do this without placing one half of myself at war with the other half; without placing my instincts at war with my reason and my reason at war with my instincts.

So, gentlemen, I appeal to all who know me to bear witness. No one can rise up and say, neither here nor anywhere else, that they have stumbled into me upon that rather crowded path of ambition. But all who have encountered me here have met me on the modest path of the good citizen. And when my days are finished, when I am lowered into my grave, it will be enough for me to be without remorse for having failed to defend a society so barbarously attacked, as well as to be without the most bitter and, for me, the intolerable pain of having done wrong to any man.

Gentlemen, in certain circumstances, in circumstances like these, I say that dictatorship is as legitimate, good, and beneficial a form of government as any other. It is a rational form of government that can be defended in theory as well as in practice. If this is not so, gentlemen, then let us examine the life of society.

Social life, like human life, is composed of action and reaction, the ebb and flow of certain invading forces as well as certain resistant forces. Such is social life as well as human life. Now, invading forces, called illnesses in the human body and something else in the social body (but essentially being one and the same thing), have two forms. In one form illnesses are completely spread throughout a society by individual persons. In the other acutely diseased form these illnesses are concentrated in and represented by political associations. Now, then, I say that the social body, like the human body, needs living resisting forces that are necessarily proportional to the state of the latter in order to repel the invading forces. When the invading forces are dispersed, so are the resisting ones. They are dispersed throughout the government, the authorities, the law courts, that is, throughout the entire social body. But when the invading forces are concentrated in political associations, then necessarily, without anyone able to impede them, without anyone having the right to impede them, the resisting forces concentrate themselves into the hands of one man. This is the clear, luminous, and indestructible theory of dictatorship.

Gentlemen, this theory, which is a truth in the rational order, is a constant fact in the historical order. Show me one society that has not had a dictatorship, only one. Look at what happened in democratic Athens and aristocratic Rome. In Athens this omnipotent power was in the hands of the people and was called ostracism. In Rome it was in the hands of the Senate, which delegated it to a worthy Consul, and was called, as in our own country, dictatorship.

Gentlemen, look at modern societies. Look at France and all of its vicissitudes. I will not speak about the First Republic, which was an enormous dictatorship without limits and full of blood and horrors. I am speaking about a later time. In the *Charter of the Restoration*,[4] dictatorship had taken refuge, or found an asylum, in Article 14. In the *Charter* of 1830 one finds it in the Preamble. What is it except a dictatorship under the nickname of Republic?

Mr. Galvez Cañero unfortunately referred here to the English Constitution. Gentlemen, it so happens that the English Constitution is the only one in the world (so wise are the English) in which dictatorship is not an exception in the law. It is in the common law. This matter is clear. The Parliament has dictatorial power on all occasions and at all times whenever it desires to exercise it. It is limited only by what limits all human powers—prudence. It is omnipotent. This is what constitutes dictatorial power. It can do everything except change a woman into a man or a man into a woman, say its jurists. It has the power to suspend the right of *habeas corpus* and to proscribe by means of a *bill of attainder.* It can change the Constitution. It can even change the dynasty, and not only the dynasty, but even the religion of the state. It can suppress consciences. It can do anything. Gentlemen, who has ever seen a more monstrous dictatorship?

I have proved that dictatorship is a theoretical truth as well as an historical fact. But now I want to say more. If I may be permitted to say this, it can be said that dictatorship is also a divine fact. Gentlemen, to a certain extent God has left the government of human societies to men and has exclusively reserved to himself the government of the universe. The universe is governed by God, if that can be said and if the expressions of parliamentary language can be applied to something so high. And, gentlemen, nothing appears more clear to me and with such strong evidence than the notion that the universe is governed by certain precise and indispensable laws called secondary causes. What are these laws if they are not analogous to those called the fundamental laws of human societies?

Now, gentlemen, if God is the legislator of the physical world, are men the legislators of human societies, but in a different way? Does God always govern by the same laws he has imposed upon himself, according to his divine wisdom, and to which he has subjected us? No, gentlemen. There are some direct, clear, and specific times when he manifests his sovereign will by breaking the laws he himself has imposed, thereby bending the natural course of things. So, gentlemen, when God operates in this way, can it not be said, if human language can be applied to divine things, that he is operating dictatorially?

Gentlemen, this proves just how great is the delirium of a party that believes it can govern with less means than God, dispensing with the use of dictatorship. But dictatorship is sometimes necessary. Gentlemen, since this is the case, the question, reduced to its real terms, does not consist in ascertaining whether dictatorship is sustainable, but whether it is good in certain circumstances. The matter consists in ascertaining whether these circumstances have arrived or passed in Spain. This is the most important point. It is on this point that I am now going to exclusively concentrate my attention. In order to do this I must cast one eye upon Europe and the other upon Spain. By doing this I will be doing nothing more than what the speakers who have preceded have done.

Gentlemen, the February Revolution[5] unexpectedly came like death. Gentlemen, God had condemned the French monarchy. In vain it profoundly transformed itself in order to accommodate itself with the circumstances and times. It was to no avail. Its condemnation was unappealable and its fall inevitable. The Monarchy of divine right ended with Louis XVI on a scaffold. The Monarchy of glory ended with Napoleon on an island. The hereditary Monarchy ended with Charles X in exile. And with Louis Philippe ended the last of all possible Monarchies—the Monarchy of prudence. It is a sad and lamentable sight, Gentlemen, when neither divine right, nor legitimacy, nor prudence, nor glory can preserve such a venerable, ancient, and glorious institution!

Gentlemen, when the news of this great revolution reached Spain, all of us were dismayed and stupefied. Nothing was comparable to our astonishment and consternation, except our consternation and astonishment over the defeated Monarchy. But that is not all. There was an even greater astonishment and consternation than when the Monarchy fell. That was over the victory of the Republic.[6] Even right now, ten months after its triumph, it must be asked how it won. We must also ask about that for which it conquered. For the Republic was the victorious instrument of a much higher power. Gentlemen, once the work of this power was begun in the destruction of the Monarchy by such a trifling thing as the Republic, the Monarchy would also be strong enough, if it was convenient and in its interests, to overthrow the Republic with such a trifling thing as the Empire or the Monarchy. Gentlemen, this revolution has been the object of great commentaries on its causes and effects in all the parliaments of Europe, particularly in the Spanish parliament. I have been amazed at the lamentable thoughtlessness with which the profound causes of revolutions have been discussed both here and elsewhere. Gentlemen, here as well as elsewhere, nothing is attributed to causing revolutions except the mistakes of governments. When catastrophes are universal, unforeseen, and simultaneous they are always something providential. Gentlemen, such are the characteristics which distinguish the works of God from the works of man.

Whenever revolutions show these symptoms, you can be sure that they come from Heaven and that they are due to our faults and for the punishment of all. Gentlemen, do you want to know the truth, the whole truth concerning the last French revolution? Well, the truth is that in February, when that great day of reckoning for all the classes of society with Providence arrived, they were found on that terrible day to be bankrupt. On that great day of reckoning with Providence, I repeat, all of them were found to be bankrupt.

Gentlemen, I will say more, that even the Republic itself, on the day of its victory, also showed itself to be bankrupt. The Republic declared that it was going to establish in the world the dominance of liberty, equality, and fraternity, three dogmas which do not come from the Republic, but from Calvary. So, gentlemen, what has happened since that time? In the name of liberty the Republic has made necessary, has proclaimed, and has accepted dictatorship. In the name of equality, in the name of republicans past and future, it has invented nothing more than a type of aristocratic democracy with a ridiculous coat of arms. And finally, gentlemen, in the name of fraternity it has restored the pagan fraternity of Eteocles and Polynices[7] with brothers devouring one another in the streets of Paris in the most enormous battle that has been seen in centuries within the walls of a city. I must contradict this Republic when it calls itself the Republic of the three truths. It is the Republic of the three blasphemies; and it is the Republic of the three lies.

Now let us proceed to the causes of this revolution. The progressive party always posits the same causes for everything. Yesterday Mr. Cortina told us that there are revolutions because of illegalities as well as because the instincts of people uniformly and spontaneously rise up against tyrants. Before that Mr. Ordax Avecilla[8] said: "If you want to avoid revolutions, then give the hungry something to eat." Now, you can see here the full extent of the theory of the progressive party. The causes of revolution, on the one hand, are misery and, on the other hand, tyranny. Gentlemen, this theory is contrary, totally contrary to History. I beg anybody to show me one single example of a revolution started and concluded by enslaved or hungry people. Revolutions are sicknesses afflicting wealthy people. And they are also sicknesses afflicting free people. In the ancient world, slaves composed the major part of the human race. Show me what revolution was every made by those slaves.

The most that they could do was to foment some slave wars. But real revolutions were always made by wealthy aristocrats. No, gentlemen, neither slavery nor misery are the germs of revolution. The germ of revolutions is found in the overexcited desires of the mob that is exploited for the benefit of its leaders. *You will be like the rich*—this is the formula of socialist revolutions against the middle classes. *You will be like the nobility*—this is the formula of the revolutions of the middle classes against the noble classes. *You will be like kings*—this is the formula of the revolutions of the noble classes against kings. Finally, gentlemen, *you shall be like gods*—this is the formula of the first rebellion of the first man against God. From Adam, the first rebel, to Proudhon, the latest impious one, this is the formula for all revolutions.

The Spanish Government was duty bound not to want that formula to be applied in Spain. It wanted it all the less because the domestic situation was not very stable. So it was necessary to take certain precautions against domestic as well as foreign contingencies. In order not to have done this it would have been necessary that the Government be unaware of every bit of power of the magnetic currents that break away from the center of revolutionary infection going about infecting the whole world.

In a few words, the domestic situation is like this: the political question was not, has never been, and is not in any way resolved. In societies so stirred up by passions, political questions cannot be easily resolved. The dynastic question was not resolved because, even if it is true that we are the victors in that matter, we did not have the resignation of victors, which is the complement of victory. The religious question was in a very bad state. The question of royal marriage, as you well know, was exasperating.

Gentlemen, I ask, as I have already shown, that if in certain circumstances dictatorship is legitimate and beneficial, were we not in such circumstances? If such circumstances had not existed, then tell me what in the world has happened that constitutes graver circumstances. Experience has shown us that the calculations of the Government and the foresight of the Congress were not unfounded. Gentlemen, all of you know this. I will speak about this only in passing, because I detest everything that feeds the passions. I did not come here for this. All of you know that he who proclaimed the Republic carried arms in the streets of Madrid. All of you know how he decorated the streets of Madrid and Seville. And all of you know that without the energetic and active resistance of the Government, all of Spain from the Pillars of Hercules[9] to the Pyrenees, from sea to sea, would have become a lake of blood. And not only Spain. Are you aware of just what sort of evils would have been propagated throughout the world if the revolution had triumphed? Ah, gentlemen, when you ponder these things you cannot help but exclaim that the Cabinet that knew how to resist and win deserves to be well praised by the Fatherland.

This question is related to the English question. Before dealing with it (and from now on I announce that I will not start something without finishing with it quickly, as I deem convenient and opportune) the Congress will permit me to expound upon some general ideas that appear expedient.

Gentlemen, I have always believed that blindness is a sign of perdition in man as well as in governments and nations. I have always believed that God always begins with blinding those whom he wants to destroy. And I believe that in order that they not see the abyss he places at their feet, he starts by confusing them. Applying these ideas to the general policies followed for some years by England and France, I will say here that I predicted many of these great misfortunes and disasters. It is a well researched and incontrovertible historical fact that the providential mission of France is to be the instrument of Providence in the propagation of new ideas, political as well as religious and social ideas.

Three great ideas have invaded Europe in modern times—the Catholic idea, the philosophical idea, and the revolutionary idea. So, gentlemen, in the three periods corresponding with these ideas, France was made man in order to propagate them. Charlemagne was France made man in order to propagate the Catholic idea; Voltaire was France made man in order to propagate the philosophical idea; Napoleon was France made man in order to propagate the revolutionary idea. Similarly, I believe that the providential mission of England, being in perpetual contrast with France, is to maintain the just moral equilibrium of the world. France is the flow and England is the ebb of the sea.

Imagine for a moment the flow without the ebb. The seas would spread themselves over every continent. Imagine the ebb without the flow. The seas would disappear from the earth. Imagine France without England. The world would not change except by means of convulsions. Every day there would be a new constitution, every hour a new government. Imagine England without France. The world would always vegetate under the charter of the venerable John Lackland,[10] which is the permanent model of all British constitutions. So then, gentlemen, what is the significance of these two powerful nations? Gentlemen, they signify limited progress through stability and vibrant stability through progress.

Gentlemen, this is how it has been for some years until today. I call upon contemporary history as well as your memories to see that these two great nations have forgotten these facts, they have forgotten their providential mission in the world. Instead of spreading new ideas throughout the world, France has everywhere preached the *status quo*—the *status quo* in France, the *status quo* in Spain, the *status quo* in Italy, and the *status quo* in the East. And instead of preaching stability, England everywhere preaches revolt—in Spain, Portugal, France, Italy, and Greece. What has been the result of this? The necessary result has been that these two nations have been badly performing rôles that have never been theirs. France has tried to convert itself from a devil into a preacher, and England from a preacher into a devil.

Gentlemen, this is contemporary history. But speaking only about England, because I propose to speak more briefly about it, I shall beseech Heaven that what has befallen France shall not befall England; that it not experience the catastrophes merited by its errors. For there is nothing comparable with the error England has made by everywhere supporting revolutionary parties. What a disgrace! Does not England know that in the day of danger these parties, with a better instinct than England's, will cut it down with swords? Has this not already happened? Gentlemen, it must happen, because every revolutionary in the world knows that when revolutions become reality, when clouds gather, when horizons are darkened, and when waves rise up, the barque of revolution has no other pilot than France.

Gentlemen, this has been the policy followed by England, or rather by the English government and its agents during recent years. I have said, and I repeat, that I do not want to deal with this question. For some rather grave considerations have moved me not to do so. First, we must consider the public good, because I solemnly declare here that I desire the most intimate alliance and the most complete union between Spain and England. England is a nation I admire and respect as being perhaps the most strong and worthy nation in the world. So, I do not want to exacerbate the matter with my words. Nor do I wish to prejudice and hinder further negotiations with that country.

There is also another consideration which has moved me not to speak about this issue. In order to speak about it I would have to become like a man with whom I was a friend, more of a friend than Mr. Cortina. But I cannot be as helpful on this matter as Mr. Cortina. Honor does not permit me to be of more help than to be silent. Permit me to speak frankly in saying that when Mr. Cortina spoke about this question he suffered from a type of vertigo. He forgot who he was, where he was, and who we are. The gentleman believed that he was a lawyer. But he was not a lawyer. He was an orator in the Parliament.

The gentleman believed that he was speaking to judges. But he was speaking to deputies. The gentleman believed that he was speaking in a court of law, but he was speaking before a deliberative assembly. He believed that he was speaking about a lawsuit, but he was speaking about a great national matter which, if it had been a lawsuit, it would have been between two nations. Now, gentlemen, was it proper for Mr. Cortina to make himself the chief prosecutor against the Spanish nation? Gentlemen, is this perhaps what is called patriotism? Is this what it is to be a patriot? No! Do you know what it is to be a patriot? To be a patriot, gentlemen, is to be one who loves, hates, and feels as our Fatherland loves, hates, and feels.

Gentlemen, he spoke about what will thoughtlessly happen concerning this matter. But what he thought will happen has already happened. Gentlemen, neither domestic affairs, which are so serious, nor foreign affairs, which are so complicated and dangerous, are enough to soften the opinion of the gentlemen who are seated in those benches. They ask about freedom. Is freedom not valued above everything else? Has not the freedom of the individual been sacrificed? Freedom, gentlemen!

Do those who proclaim this sacred word understand the principle they proclaim and the name they pronounce? Do they understand the times in which they live? Gentlemen, has not the noise of the latest disasters reached your ears? Don't you know that now freedom is finished? Have you not followed its sorrowful passion, as I have with my own eyes? Gentlemen, have you not seen it harassed, mocked, and treacherously wounded by all the demagogues of the world? Have you not seen it raised up in anguish over the mountains of Switzerland or along the banks of the Seine, the Rhine, the Danube, or the Tiber? Have you not seen it ascend to its Calvary on the Quirinal?

Gentlemen, these words are terrible. But we must not retreat from uttering them if they express the truth, which I am resolved to speak. Freedom is dead! Gentlemen, it will not rise again on the third day, nor in the third year, nor perhaps in three centuries! So, gentlemen, are you frightened of the tyranny we now suffer? If you are, you are frightened of something small. You will see even worse things. Gentlemen, here I ask you to fix my words in your memory, because what I am about to tell you is going to happen to the letter. The events I am going to predict are in a future that is nearer to than farther from us.

Gentlemen, the foundation of all your errors consists in not knowing the direction that civilization and the world are taking. You believe that civilization and the world are progressing, when they are actually regressing. Gentlemen, the world is moving rapidly towards the establishment of a despotism, the greatest and most devastating despotism in the memory of man. Civilization and the world are moving in this direction. I do not need to be a prophet in order to say these things. It is merely enough for me to consider this dreadful conjunction of human events from the only true point of view—from the Catholic heights.

Gentlemen, there are no more than two possible forms of repression. One is internal and the other external—religious and political. They are of such a nature that when the religious thermometer rises, the thermometer of political repression falls. And when the religious thermometer falls, the political thermometer—political repression, tyranny—rises. This is a law of humanity, a law of History. If it is not, gentlemen, then look about at the world. Look at the state of society in the times before the Cross. Tell me what existed when there was no internal repression, when there was no religious repression. What existed was a society of tyrants and slaves. Show me a single people from that time who were neither slaves nor tyrants.

This is an indisputable fact, a fact even recognized by the Socialists. Yes, they admit this. They call Jesus a divine man. But they go even further. They claim that they are his successors. Holy God, his successors! These men of blood and vengeance, the successors of him who lived only in order to do good; who did not perform miracles except in order to free sinners from sin and the dead from death; who in the space of three years carried out the greatest revolution that has ever taken place in the world. And that was done without shedding any blood other than his own.

Gentlemen, I beg you to give me your attention. I am going to present you with the most amazing parallel that History has to offer. You have seen that in the ancient world, when religious repression was lowest, because it did not exist, political repression was at its highest because it became tyrannical. Very well then, with Jesus Christ, when religious repression is born, political repression completely disappears. This is so certain, that when Jesus Christ founded a society with his disciples, it was the only society that existed without a government. Between Jesus and his disciples there was no other government than the love of the Master for his disciples and of his disciples for their Master. It can be said that when internal repression was complete, freedom was absolute.

Let us follow the parallel. The apostolic times have arrived, which I shall extend, for the purposes of my proposal, from the apostolic times, properly speaking, until the rise of Christianity in the Capitol in the time of Constantine the Great.[11] At that time, gentlemen, the Christian religion, that is to say, internal religious repression, was at its high point. But, even though it was at its high point, something happened that happens to all societies composed of men. A germ began to develop, nothing more than the germ of license and religious freedom. So, gentlemen, observe the parallel. A rise in the political thermometer corresponds from the start with the lowering of the religious thermometer. There is not yet any government. A government is not necessary. But the germ of a government is already necessary. In the Christian society of that time there was no real need for magistrates. Yet there were arbitrating judges and other arbitrators who formed the embryo of a government. It was really no more than this. The Christians of apostolic times did not engage in lawsuits and never had recourse to courts of law. They decided their disputes through arbitration. Observe, gentlemen, how the growth of government goes along with the increase of corruption.

Now come the feudal times. Here religion is still encountered at its pinnacle, but is vitiated by human passions. Gentlemen, what happened at that time in the political world? A real and effective government was already needed. But it was enough that it was of the most weak kind. So the feudal monarchy was established, the weakest of all monarchies.

Let us still follow our parallel. Gentlemen, the sixteenth century has arrived. In this century, with the great Lutheran reform, with this great scandal that was political and social as well as religious, with this act of intellectual and moral emancipation, coincided the rise of the following institutions. The feudal monarchies became absolute monarchies. Gentlemen, you believe that a monarchy cannot be anything more than absolute. How can a government be more absolute?

Gentlemen, it was necessary, though, that the thermometer of political repression rise more because the religious thermometer continued falling. In fact, it rose even more. And what new institution was created? That of permanent armies. Gentlemen, do you know what permanent armies are? In order to know this it is enough to know what a soldier is. A soldier is a slave with a uniform. So you see once more, at the moment when religious repression falls, political repression rises as high as absolutism, or even higher. It was not enough for governments to be absolute. They asked for, and obtained, the privilege of being absolute and of having a million arms.

In spite of this, gentlemen, it was necessary that the political thermometer rise even more because the religious thermometer continued to fall. Gentlemen, what new institution was then created? Governments said: "We have a million arms. But that is not enough. We need something else. We need a million eyes." So they obtained police, and with the police a million eyes. In spite of this, gentlemen, the political thermometer and political repression still had to rise because, despite everything, the religious thermometer continued falling. And so it rose.

Then, gentlemen, it was not enough for governments to have a million arms and a million eyes. They wanted to have a million ears. So they devised administrative centralization. Through this form of administration, all claims and complaints reached the governments. However, gentlemen, that was not enough because the religious thermometer continued to fall. So it was necessary that the political thermometer rise even more. And so it rose.

Governments said: "A million arms, a million eyes, and a million ears are not enough for the task of repression. We need more. We need to have the privilege of being everywhere at the same time." So they obtained this privilege. The telegraph was invented. Gentlemen, this was the state of Europe and the world when the first outburst of the last revolution announced to everyone that there is still not enough despotism in the world just because the religious thermometer was below zero. So, gentlemen, we have a choice to make between two things.

I have promised to speak today with complete frankness. And I shall keep my word. Well now, this is the choice we must make. Either there will be a religious reaction or there will not be one. You will soon see, gentlemen, that as the religious thermometer rises the political thermometer will fall naturally and spontaneously, without any effort on the part of people, governments, or men, until that warm day when all nations are free. But if, on the contrary, gentlemen (it is not customary to call such matters to the attention of deliberative assemblies, and I believe that in your benevolence you will also indulge me), I say that if the religious thermometer continues falling, no one can know where we are finally going to be. Gentlemen, I do not know where we are going, and I tremble when I think about it. Consider the analogies that I have placed before you. If government was not necessary when religious repression was at its height, and now that religious repression does not exist, there will be no form of government powerful enough to maintain order, for all despotisms will be weak.

Gentlemen, this is placing the finger in the wound. This is the matter now before Spain, Europe, humanity, and the whole world.

Gentlemen, consider one thing. In the ancient world tyranny was fierce and devastating. Yet this tyranny was principally limited because states were small and international relations between them were totally impossible. Consequently, in ancient times tyrannies of a grand scale were impossible, except for one—Rome. But now, gentlemen, how things have changed! Gentlemen, the way is prepared for an enormous, colossal, universal, and immense tyranny. Everything is prepared for it. Gentlemen, look well. There is already neither physical nor moral resistance to it. There is no physical resistance because with the electric telegraph there are no distances. And there is no moral resistance because all souls are divided and all patriotism is dead. Tell me now whether or not I am correct when I am preoccupied with the immediate future of the world. Tell me if, when dealing with this question, I am not dealing with the true question.

One thing, and only one thing, can avoid a disaster. We cannot avoid it by granting more freedom, more guarantees, and new constitutions. This can only be avoided if all of us, as far as our strength can reach, provoke a healthy religious reaction. Now, gentlemen, is this reaction possible? It is possible, but is it probable? Gentlemen, here I speak with the deepest sadness. I do not believe that it is probable. Gentlemen, I have seen and known many individuals who have left the Faith and have returned to it. Unfortunately, Gentlemen, I have never seen a people return to it after they have lost it.

If any hope remained in me, it was lost, gentlemen, due to the recent events in Rome. And now I am going to say a few words about this matter, which has also been discussed by Mr. Cortina. Gentlemen, there is no word for the events that have occurred in Rome. What word would you use, gentlemen? Would you call them deplorable? All of the events I have just discussed are deplorable. It is much worse than that. Would you call these events horrible? Gentlemen, these events go beyond every horror. There was in Rome someone who is no longer there. He is the most just and evangelical man in the world. And he sits on the most eminent throne. What has Rome done to this most evangelical and just man? What has this city, where heroes, Cæsars, and Pontiffs ruled, done? It has exchanged the throne of Pontiffs for the throne of demagogues. Rebellious against God, it has fallen into the idolatry of the dagger. This is what Rome has done. The dagger, gentlemen, the demagogic and bloody dagger is today the idol of Rome. This is the idol which overthrew Pius IX.[12] This is the idol that the Caribbean mobs are parading in the streets. Did I say Caribbeans? I spoke badly, because Caribbeans may be fierce, but they are not ungrateful.

Gentlemen, I have proposed to speak with complete frankness. And I shall so speak. I say that it is necessary for the King of Rome to return to Rome or, with all due respect to Mr. Cortina, no stone will remain standing there. The Catholic world cannot, and will not, consent to the virtual destruction of Christianity by a single city being handed over to a frenzy of madness. Gentlemen, civilized Europe cannot, and will not, consent to the collapse of the cupola of the edifice of European civilization. Gentlemen, the world cannot, and will not, consent to the accession in the Holy City of a new and strange dynasty to the throne, the dynasty of crime. And let it not be said, gentlemen, as Mr. Cortina and the newspapers and speeches of the gentlemen seated on those benches have said, that two questions are at stake here—one temporal and one spiritual. And also let it not be said that the matter here is between a temporal king and his people. The Pontiff still lives. Gentlemen, only a few words will explain everything here.

Without a doubt, spiritual power is the principle attribute of the Pope. Temporal power is only accessory to it. But this accessory is necessary. The Catholic world has the right to expect that the infallible oracle of its dogmas be free and independent. And the Catholic world can only be certain that this oracle is independent and free when it is sovereign, because only a sovereign is dependent upon no one.

Consequently, gentlemen, the question concerning sovereignty, which is everywhere a political matter, is moreover a religious matter in Rome. The people, who can be sovereign everywhere else, cannot be sovereign in Rome. Constituent assemblies that can exist everywhere else cannot exist in Rome. In Rome there can be no other constituent power except the power already constituted there. Gentlemen, Rome and the Papal States[13] do not belong to Rome. And they do not belong to the Pope. The Papal States belong to the Catholic world. The Catholic world has recognized them so that the Pope may be independent and free. The Pope himself cannot despoil himself of this sovereignty and independence.

Gentlemen, I am going to conclude because the Congress is tired, and so am I. Frankly, gentlemen, I must declare here that I cannot continue because I am ill. It is a miracle that I could speak at all. But the most important thing is that I have already said what I needed to say.

After having discussed the three foreign matters that were dealt with by Mr. Cortina, I return, in conclusion, to domestic affairs. Gentlemen, ever since the beginning of the world until now it has been debated whether or not resistance or concession are proper in order to avoid revolutions and upheavals. But fortunately, gentlemen, what has been a question since the first year of creation until 1848, in the year of grace 1848, is no longer a question because the matter has been resolved. Gentlemen, if my illness would permit me, I would like to review all of the events from February until now in order to prove this claim. But I shall content myself with recalling only two of these events.

In France, gentlemen, the Monarchy offered no resistance and was conquered by the Republic, which barely had enough power to set itself in motion. And this Republic, which barely had enough power to set itself in motion, conquered socialism because it resisted.

In Rome, the other example I want to mention, what has happened? Tell me, if you had been artists and wanted to paint the model of a king, would you have chosen Pius IX as your model? Gentlemen, Pius IX tried to be magnificent and generous, like his divine Master. He found outlaws in his country. He gave them his hand and allowed them to return to their homeland. Gentlemen, there were reformers, and he granted them the reforms they sought. There were liberals, gentlemen. And he granted them freedom. Every word of his was of some benefit. Now, gentlemen, answer this question for me. Are the ignominies he now suffers not equal to, even more than, the benefits he bestowed? And in view of this, gentlemen, is this not a result of granting concessions?

Gentlemen, if it was only a question here of choosing between freedom, on one side, and dictatorship, on the other side, there would be no disagreement. After being embraced by freedom, who could kneel down before a dictatorship? But this is not the problem. Freedom, in fact, does not exist in Europe. The constitutional governments that represented it these past few years are everywhere nothing more, gentlemen, than frameworks. They are skeletons without life.

Remember one thing, remember Imperial Rome. Every republican institution existed in Rome. There were omnipotent dictators, inviolable tribunes, and eminent consuls. Gentlemen, all this existed. Only one thing was lacking. One man was not wanted. And that is what the Republic lacked.

Gentlemen, this is the situation of almost all the constitutional governments in Europe. Mr. Cortina unwittingly demonstrated this to us the other day. Did he not tell us, and with good reason, that he prefers what History has to say, rather than what theories say? Therefore, it is to History that I appeal. Mr. Cortina, what are these governments with their legitimate majorities, with their responsible ministers who respond to nothing, with their inviolable kings who are always violated? As I have said, gentlemen, the choice is not between freedom and dictatorship. If this was the choice, I would vote for freedom, like every single one of us seated here. But, I conclude, this is the problem. One must deal with choosing between a dictatorship of insurrection and a dictatorship of the Government. Placed in this situation, I choose the dictatorship of the Government as the least wearisome as well as the least outrageous.

One must choose between a dictatorship that comes from below and one that comes from above. I choose the one from above because it comes from the most clean and serene regions. Finally, one must choose between a dictatorship of the dagger and a dictatorship of the saber. I choose the dictatorship of the saber because it is more noble. Gentlemen, by voting we shall divide ourselves on this question, and in so doing, we shall consequently be divided among ourselves. Gentlemen, you will vote as always, following the most popular course. We, gentlemen, as always, will vote for what is more healthy.

NOTES

1. Manuel Cortina (1802–1862), was a leader of the Spanish revolution of 1840, a prominent and leading member of the Progressive Party in the Cortes, and a leader of the Madrid Radical Junta. See H. Butler Clarke, *Modern Spain: 1815–1898* (New York: AMS Press, 1969), pp. 148, 159, 164, 165, 167, 168, 172, 175, 179,

184; Ramon Menéndez Pidal, *Historia de España: la era Isabelina y el sexenio democrático (1834–1874)*, vol. XXXIV (Madrid: Espasa Calpe, 1981), pp. 373, 376, 388, 412, 415, 416, 441, 443, 447. The Cortes was organized according to the various political parties or factions. The principle political factions this time were the Progressives (*Progeresistas*), the Moderates (*Moderados*), and the Carlists (*Carlistas*). The Progressives included the old radicals that supported the liberal reforms of 1812. The Moderates were constitutional monarchists made up of a coalition of the conservative supporters of Queen Isabel II and various moderates. The Carlists were an ultra-conservative and ultra-Catholic faction supporting the return of a traditional and Catholic monarchy and social order and a rival claimant to the Spanish throne, Carlos, brother of Ferdinand VII and uncle of Isabel II. See Graham, ibid., pp. 44-51; Edgar Holt, *The Carlist Wars in Spain* (Chester Springs: Dufour Editions, 1967), pp. 39, 51, 143, 149, 206, 217.

2. This speech was delivered in the Cortes on 4 January 1849 in response to speeches by Manuel Cortina and José Ordax Avecilla denouncing excesses of repression by the Narváez régime.

3. Donoso was speaking on behalf of the government and the conservative faction in the Cortes.

4. This formalized the restoration of the Bourbon monarchy in France. The restored monarchy was overthrown by a revolution in February 1848.

5. This is the revolution of 1848 that broke out in France. Germany, Austria, Hungary, and Italy were also engulfed in revolution during the same year.

6. The Second French Republic.

7. See Sophocles, *Antigone*.

8. José Ordax Avecilla (1813–1856), prominent leader of the left wing of the Progressive Party in the Cortes (1843–1849), member of a socialist circle in Madrid inspired by the ideas of the French socialist Charles Fourier, and a founder of the Democratic Republican Party in 1849. See V. G. Kiernan, *The Revolution of 1854 in Spanish History* (Oxford: Clarendon, 1966), pp. 31, 42, 64, 69, 83, 106, 120, 129, 173, 241; Menéndez Pidal, *Historia de España*, pp. 270, 271, 291, 418, 419, 490, 492, 493, 496–498, 802.

9. The Straits of Gibralter.

10. John I (1167–1216), king of England, promulgated the *Magna carta* in 1215.

11. Under the emperor Constantine, Christianity became the state religion of the Roman Empire in the fourth century C.E.

12. Pope Pius IX (1792–1878) began his pontificate (1846–1878) by making some liberal reforms in the Papal States. He fled Rome during the revolution of 1848. After the revolution he became a key figure in the conservative reaction against liberalism and socialism. In his fight against these trends he issued the encyclical *Quanta cura* and the *Syllabus of Errors* in 1864 wherein liberalism, socialism, rationalism, democracy, freedom of thought, freedom of speech, and other ideas associated with the Enlightenment and its aftermath were condemned. In 1871, during the First Vatican Council, he promulgated the doctrine of papal infallibility.

13. The Papal States were a political entity in central Italy ruled directly by the Pope dating back to the late Middle Ages. They were overthrown and incorporated into the Kingdom of Italy in 1871.

Letters to the Count of Montalembert

Berlin, 26 May 1849

Dear Sir:

Knowing that you understand Spanish, I have taken the liberty to answer your most appreciated letter of 7 May in my own tongue, since it is not possible for me to express my thoughts properly with clarity and fluency in a foreign language.

The election season was beginning when you so kindly wrote me. Considering that this and my desire not to be distracted during such an important time dissuaded me from answering you until now, I have made good use of the interval between the last electoral activities and the first discussions of the legislative Assembly.

The sympathy of a man like you is the most beautiful earthly recompense of my honest efforts to uphold in the highest degree the Catholic, conservative, and vivifying principle of human societies. Apart from this, I will respond fittingly to the benevolent sympathy that you have shown me if I do not present myself as I am before your eyes, or as I believe myself to be, with the truth in my mouth and with my heart in my hand. This is especially necessary since I have not taken the occasion until now to say everything that I think about the most grave problems which today occupy the most eminent geniuses.

The destiny of humanity is a profound mystery that has received two contrary explanations: one Catholic and the other philosophical. The ensemble of every one of these explanations constitutes a complete civilization. Between these two civilizations there is an unfathomable abyss, an absolute antagonism. The attempts directed at trying to achieve a compromise between them have been, are, and will always be vain. One is error; the other is truth. One is evil; the other is good. It is necessary to choose between them firmly and decisively, and everywhere proclaim the one while condemning the other after the choice has been made. Those who fluctuate between them, those who accept the principles of the one and the consequences of the other, end up parting company with great minds and are unpardonably condemned to absurdity.

I believe that Catholic civilization is good without any evil mixed with it. And philosophy is evil without any good mixed with it. Catholic civilization teaches that human nature is sick and fallen; radically fallen and sick in its essence and in all the elements that constitute it. Since human understanding is sick, it can neither invent nor discover the truth, except when it is placed before it. Since the will is sick, it can neither desire nor do good unless it is helped. And it cannot be helped unless it is subjugated and repressed. Since this is the case, it is clear that freedom of discussion necessarily leads to error, just as freedom of action necessarily leads to evil. Human reason cannot see the truth if it is not shown to it by an infallible teaching authority. The human will can neither desire nor do good if it is not repressed by the fear of God. When the will is emancipated from God and reason emancipated from the Church, error and evil reign without counterweight in the world.

Philosophical civilization teaches that human nature is sound and healthy; radically healthy and whole in its essence and in the elements that constitute it. Since the understanding of man is healthy, it can see, discover, and invent truth. Since the will is healthy, it can naturally desire and do good. Supposing this, it is clear that reason will arrive at knowing the truth, all the truth, if left to itself. And the will, if left to itself, necessarily will realize the absolute good. So, it is clear that the solution to the great social problem lies in breaking all the bonds that restrain and subjugate human reason and free will. Evil is neither in the free will nor reason, but in those bonds. If evil consists in having bonds, and goodness in not having them, then perfection will consist in not having bonds of any sort. If this is true, humanity will be perfect when it rejects God, who is the divine bond; and when it rejects Government, which is the political bond; and when it rejects property, which is the social bond; and when it rejects the family, which is the domestic bond. All who do not accept each and every one of these conclusions, and all who place themselves outside of this civilization, while not entering the Catholic fraternity, walk in the deserts of a vacuum.

Let us proceed from the theoretical problem to the practical one. What do these two civilizations promise in the time of victory? I respond to this question, without my pen wavering, without my heart being oppressed, and without my reason being disturbed, by saying that the triumph in time will irremissibly go to philosophical civilization. Has man desired freedom? Indeed, yes. Has he abhorred bonds? All of them have fallen in pieces at his feet. There was a day when, in order to take the pulse of his freedom, he wanted to kill his God. Did he not do that? Did he not put him on a cross and place him between two thieves? Did not the angels, perhaps, come down from heaven in order to defend the just, who suffered on the earth? So, why do they not come down now, when we are not dealing with the crucifixion of God, but with the crucifixion of man by man? Why do they not now descend, when our consciences are telling our voices that in this great tragedy no one merits their intervention, not even those who have been the victims or the executioners.

Here we are dealing with a more serious question. We are trying to investigate nothing less than the true spirit of Catholicism concerning the vicissitudes of this enormous battle between evil and goodness, or, as St. Augustine said, between the city of God and the earthly city. I think it is proved and evident that evil always triumphs over good here below, and that the triumph over evil is something reserved to God personally, if that can be said.

For this reason there is no historical period which has not ended in a great catastrophe. The first historical period began with creation and ended in a deluge. And what is meant by the deluge? The deluge means two things: the natural triumph of evil over good and the supernatural triumph of God over evil by means of a *direct*, *personal*, and *sovereign* action.

Men, still drenched by the waters of the deluge, commenced the struggle again. Darkness covered all horizons. Everything was dark when the Lord came. The fog was evident. The Lord was raised upon the cross, and daylight returned to the world. What is meant by this great catastrophe? It means two things: It signifies the natural triumph of evil over good and the supernatural triumph of God over evil by means of a *direct*, *personal*, and *sovereign* action.

This is philosophy for me, the whole philosophy of History. Vico[1] was ready to see the truth, and if he had seen it, he would have explained it better than me. But having quickly lost the luminous line, he returned to the darkness. In the infinite variety of human successes, he believed that a certain and restricted number of political and social forms always could be discovered. In order to demonstrate his error it is enough to look at the United States, which does not conform to any of these forms. If he had entered more profoundly into the Catholic mysteries, he would have seen that the truth in this proposition is the other way around. The truth is in the substantial identity of the successes, guarded and hidden by the infinite variety of forms.

Since this is what I believe, I leave it to you to guess my opinion over the result of the battle that is joined today in the world. I have not said that if the victory is sure, then the fight is over, because, in the first place, the struggle can postpone the catastrophe and, secondly, the struggle is a duty and not a speculation for those whom we consider Catholics. Let us give thanks to God for giving us the fight. And let us not ask for anything except the grace to fight and triumph which, in his infinite goodness, he reserves for those who fight well for his cause as a greater recompense than victory.

Regarding the manner of combat, I encounter nothing more today than something which can give useful results. The combat is by means of the printed newspaper. Today it is necessary that the truth be spoken into the ear and that it resounds in it monotonously and perpetually, so that its echoes have to arrive at that hidden sanctuary where enervated and sleeping souls are lying. The battles of the tribune count for little.

Speeches, being frequent, do not charm. If they are rare, they leave no impression upon the memory. The applause which is wrested is not triumphal because it is for the artist, not for the Christian. Among all the newspapers today that see the light in France, *L'Univers*[2] is the one that appears to me to have exercised, above all in these times, the most healthy and beneficial influence.

In this sort of general confession which I am making to you, I must declare here guilelessly that my political and religious ideas today do not seem to be like my political and religious ideas of another time. My conversion to good principles owes itself, in the first place, to divine mercy, and then, to the deep study of revolutions. Revolutions are the lighthouses of Providence and of History. Those who have had the fortune or the disgrace of living and dying in calm and peaceful times, can be said to have run through life arriving at death without leaving infancy. Only those who, like us, live in the midst of torments, can dress themselves in the cloak of virility and say to themselves that they are men.

Considered in a certain way, revolutions, like heresies, are good because they confirm and clarify the faith. I had never understood the enormous rebellion of Lucifer, until I saw with my own eyes the senseless pride of Proudhon. Human blindness almost has become a mystery in the light of the incurable and supernatural blindness of the accommodated classes. In the light of the dogma of the innate perversion of human nature and of the inclination to evil, who can doubt it today if one looks at the socialist phalanx?

It is time to end this letter, which does not need a reply, since it is nothing more than the relief of an idle man directed to a busy man. When I have the pleasure of seeing you, let us occupy ourselves more thoroughly with these great problems. Then I will have the pleasure of receiving from your own hands the collection of your most eloquent speeches, a precious gift for those who, like me, esteem your noble character and admire your illustrious talent.

In the meantime, I remain your attentive and sure servant.

—The Marquis of Valdegamas

Berlin, 4 June 1849

My dear Count:

I just received this very day your letter of 1 June in response to my letter to you of 26 May. The agreement of our ideas is one of the most flattering things to me. Your friendship and sympathy are also inestimable, and I value this greatly.

Our agreement goes further than and is more absolute than it seems to you. Catholic civilization can be considered in two different ways: in itself as a certain ensemble of religious and social principles or as an historical reality, in which these principles are linked to human freedom. Considered from the first point of view, Catholic civilization, in its development in time and its extension in space, is subject to the imperfections and vicissitudes of all that is extended in space and prolonged in time. In my letter I will only deal with this civilization from the perspective of the first point of view. Considering it from the perspective of the second viewpoint, that is, in its historical reality, I will say that since its imperfections were born solely from its linkage with freedom, true human progress consists in subjugating the human element, the one that corrupts, to that which purifies—the divine.

Society has followed another course. It has brought an end to the rule of faith proclaiming the independence of reason and the will of man. It has converted evil, which was relative, exceptional, and contingent, into a universal and necessary absolute. This period of rapid decline in Europe began with the restoration of pagan literature, which then successively produced the restoration of pagan philosophy, pagan religion, and pagan politics. Today the world is in the eve of the last of these restorations, the restoration of pagan socialism.

History is already at the stage of forming its judgment about these two great civilizations, one in which the reason and will of man conforms to the divine element, and the other, which sets aside the divine element and proclaims the independence and sovereignty of the human element. The golden age of Catholic civilization, that is, the age in which the reason and will of man conformed more perfectly to the divine, or, to the Catholic element (which is the same as the divine), was, without a doubt, the fourteenth century. So the iron age of philosophical civilization, that is, the age in which the reason and will of man arrived at the high point of its independence and sovereignty is, without a doubt, the nineteenth century.

Apart from this, this great decline was written into the law, known and at the same time mysterious, by which God directs and governs the human race. If Catholic civilization had followed a path of continuous progress, the earth would have become a paradise for man. But God wanted the world to be a valley of tears. If God had been a socialist, what would Proudhon have been? Everyone is exactly where he should be. God is in Heaven and Proudhon is in the world. Proudhon will always be seeking, without ever finding, a paradise in a valley of tears. And God places this great valley between two great paradises so that man might live between a great hope and a great memory.

Going now to the request you made of me in the name of the editors of *L'Univers* concerning the publication of my letter, I must say to you that in other times it had been greatly undesirable. But today that is no longer the case. I have held that literary perfectionism, that is, perfectionism in expression and beauty in form, and the forms of a particular letter are neither literary nor beautiful. But this perfectionism has passed away. Today I scorn more than admire this talent, which is a nervous infirmity more than a talent of the soul.

When I have the pleasure of seeing you we shall speak more fully about these matters. These quick remarks are enough for a letter.

In the meantime, I remain your attentive and sure servant.

—The Marquis of Valdegamas

NOTES

1. Giambattista Vico (1668–1744), historical philosopher who attempted to systematize the humanities into a single human science in a cyclical theory of the growth and decline of societies.

2. *L'Univers*, published by Louis Veuillot, was the most influential Ultramontanist Catholic publication in France in the nineteenth century.

Letter to the Editors of *El Pais* and *El Heraldo*

Berlin, 16 July 1849

My dear friends:

In the newspapers that you publish[1] you printed two articles in which civility competed with genius in response to the letters I had the honor of writing to the Count of Montalembert. There was a time when I was an obstinate jouster in intellectual contests. That time, however, has already passed since I have become convinced that controversies are of little value. They serve, rather, more to hinder than enliven the human race on its rapturous path. The ages of disputes are the ages of sophists. And the ages of sophists are ages of great decadence. After the sophists always come the barbarians, sent by God in order to cut the thread of argument with their swords.

I have resolved, therefore, not to do this today out of respect for our friendship and in order to give a public testimony of my appreciation to you and of the homage I am disposed to render to your illustrious talents.

Now I will say something that can be said concerning the observations you made about my letters. Since I do not have enough time in order to send a separate letter to both publications, I am sending only one letter to the publication that was the first to impugn me. I ask the other paper, if it sees fit, to insert my letter in its columns, since it addresses both publications. At the same time I must declare, with pen in hand, that I will also answer any other papers if others have honored me with their opposition. Silence must be attributed to me regarding them because I have only received *El Pais*, *La España*, and *El Heraldo*.

One of you accused me of Manichæism and of belonging to the neo-Catholic school of thought. Concerning the latter accusation, I must say that, first, I do not know if such a school of thought exists; second, if it exists, I am ignorant of what it says; third, even if it does exist, I do not belong to it. I am a pure Catholic. I believe and profess what is believed and professed by the Catholic, apostolic, and Roman Church. I do not look to philosophers in order for me to know what I must believe and think. I look to the Church's doctors. I do not ask anything of learned thinkers because they cannot answer me. It is better for me to put my questions to pious women and children, both vessels of blessing, because the one is purified with tears while the other is always scented with the perfume of innocence.

I see two great edifices, two Babylonian towers, two splendid civilizations raised up by human wisdom. The first fell before the sound of apostolic trumpets. The second one fell before the sound of socialist trumpets. In the presence of this tremendous spectacle, I ask myself in terror if human reason is nothing more than vanity and a spiritual affliction. I am not unaware that there are men with an invincible optimism for whom it is evident that society does not have to fall because it has already fallen. Their eyes, far from being open, are darkened like the clouds that float through the air. The February revolution was a punishment for them. What comes next will be an act of mercy. Those who are alive will see, and those who see will be astonished at seeing, that the February revolution was nothing more than a menace and that chastisement now follows it.

It would be a very serious matter if the accusation against me of Manichæism was well grounded. Manichæans, in modern as well as in ancient times, have afflicted the Church with scandals and have heaped tribulations upon its bitter heart. Nevertheless, the accusation against me is totally unfounded.

If the coexistence of evil and good is enough to constitute Manichæism, then the Church would be Manichæan because it proclaims, like the books of the Bible and in one voice with its doctors, that evil and good exist side by side in the world. If the struggle between good and evil is enough to constitute Manichæism, the Church would be Manichæan because it proclaims, like the books of the Bible and in one voice with its doctors, that this struggle has existed since the beginning of that great tragedy in paradise. And it will extend through all times. If the *natural* victory of evil over good is enough to constitute Manichæism, the Church would be Manichæan because it proclaims, like the books of the Bible and in one voice with its doctors, that good can only triumph miraculously. The flood, in which good was victorious over evil, was a miracle. And the final judgment, in which good will triumph over evil forever, is like the crown of all miracles.

What is done by human societies, as well as by individuals, is subject to the same law, even if it correctly operates among them in a different manner. Evil triumphs over the individual man just as it triumphs over society—*naturally*. And it is not conquered in either man or society except by means of a miraculous influence. That miraculous influence on man is called *grace*. And *grace*, which is the principle of *justification* in man, is at the same time the principle of victory.

There is this similarity between the salvation of societies and the salvation of individual men. Both are accomplished by a miracle. But there is this difference. In man the miracle is commonly internal and invisible, while in society it is external. It can even be said that it is palpable. God speaks to man without words. He speaks loudly to the world.

Now, the notion of evil existing at the side of good is not Manichæan. And the notion of a struggle between good and evil is not Manichæan. Furthermore, there is nothing Manichæan in the notion that the victory of evil over good is accomplished by *natural* means.

So, who can be considered a Manichæan? I could be considered a Manichæan if I proposed an existence, independent of the will of God, to the ravages of evil, and if I had made a god of it rivaling the Most High God, engaging him in a monumental battle over who must dominate Heaven and earth, rule over the visible and the invisible, and rule over angels and men. Such a blasphemy has neither been in my heart nor come from my lips.

Lucifer is not the rival, but the slave of the Most High. The evil that inspires and infuses neither infuses nor inspires unless the Lord permits it. And the Lord does not permit this except in order to punish the impious and purify the just with the red-hot iron of tribulations. This is the way evil itself is transformed into good under the omnipotent entreaty of him who has no equal in power, greatness, and wonder. He is who he is. And it is he who casts everything that is opposed to him into the abyss of nothingness.

I still have a deeper objection, because it is said that the consequence that can result from my opinion concerning the irremissible triumph of evil not only attacks Catholicism, but also Christianity, since the mission of Christ would be declared virtually insufficient in this case.

There are two serious errors here. One concerns my opinion and the other one concerns the mission of the Savior of the human race. It is simply untrue that I believe the triumph of evil to be irremissible. I have expressly said the contrary. Good triumphed over evil in the flood. It triumphed over evil with the arrival of the Lord. And in the final judgment it will triumph over evil, and its triumph will be endless because time will be finished. For there is no time in eternity.

All that I have said is that evil *naturally* triumphs over good. And this, besides being something that cannot be doubted, is also something that conforms with Catholic doctrine. Catholicism does not say that man must be powerful in order to triumph over evil. It says exactly the opposite of this, because it teaches that societies cannot triumph over evil unless they are helped by the arm of God. And man cannot triumph over it unless he is aided by grace. I affirm, on the one hand, the *natural* triumph of evil over good as well as, on the other hand, the *supernatural* triumph of God over evil. I have done nothing but reduce the great principles of Catholicism to a brief and comprehensive formula, basing it on the omnipotence of God and the frailty of man.

I shall now proceed to the error concerning the mission of Our Lord Jesus Christ. I say that Jesus Christ is not called and is not the Savior because he saved all men. He is called and is the Savior because no one could be saved before his arrival on earth. After his arrival all *could* be saved, if they so desired. Concerning the first point, it is known that the just under the old law in the bosom of Abraham were expecting him and could not leave that bosom in order to go to Heaven until they were redeemed by Christ's most precious blood. Concerning the second point, the text of the evangelist is quite clear: "He came unto his own: and his own received him not. But as many as received him, he gave them power to be made the sons of God, to them that believe in his name. Who are born, not of blood, nor of the will of the flesh, nor of the will of man, but of God."[2]

In summary, in order for this doctrine to remain so clear, like the sun that shines on us, the mystery of our redemption is reduced principally to the reestablishment of the happy equilibrium of human freedom, shattered by sin, through the merits of our Savior and by his grace.

Men have been through three different stages of development. In the first stage they were completely free, and their freedom consisted in the power that was given to them to choose between saving or losing themselves. By losing themselves, they entered the second stage. What distinguishes this stage from the first stage is that instead of possessing complete freedom, men possessed only a diminished freedom. Men could not save themselves. But they could lose themselves. Their freedom fell into the same abyss into which their innocence fell.

With the arrival of the Lord, they passed into the third stage. Here they recovered their primitive freedom by means of grace, which was given to men in a sufficient degree through the merits of Our Lord Jesus Christ, whose most precious blood washed away the stain of sin. *Ubi abundavit delictum, ibi gratia superabundavit* (Where sin abounds, there grace is superabundant). With grace men recovered their complete freedom. And with their complete freedom they recovered their power of choosing between losing and saving themselves.

A man can take any one of these two roads. He can take the road to perdition, without his definitive perdition enabling him to rise up against God, just as Adam was unable to do in that first fall. A man is free, sovereignly free, in the presence of his God, whose reverence for human freedom is confined within his most profound designs as well as in his most sublime works. Free will is so inviolable and so holy that neither God nor man can impede anyone from taking the greatest as well as the most terrible actions involving his freedom.

This is the act in which a man kills himself and loses his soul—suicide and sin. There is no freedom that has ever been or can be taken away by a tyrant, not even freedom *par excellence*, which is outside the jurisdiction of tyrants. Everything can be done to me, everything. But I cannot be forced to live if I abhor life. And I cannot be carried by force to the gate of salvation if I do not want to be saved.

See how the question of the future of human societies can be widely considered without any of the possible solutions being contrary to Catholicism. This is a question of freedom. You can only try to investigate whether human societies, on the road they freely take, shall end up being perfect or dead. It can be said that you are convinced that they shall be perfect. I am regrettably convinced that they shall die.

Moreover, I say that my solution, without being accepted and defined by the Church, without being formally articulated in the Sacred Scriptures, and without having been expressly sustained by the Church's doctors, is, however, completely in conformity with the internally diffused spirit of the Catholic religion.

Follow along with me in the footsteps of the Savior, from the moment of his birth in the manger until his death on the cross. What is the meaning of this cloud of sadness that perpetually covers his most sacred face? The people of Galilee had seen him weep. Jerusalem saw his face inundated with tears. Who ever saw him laugh? And what was it that passed so disturbingly before those eyes that saw everything, the present as well as the past, the past as well as the future? Did those eyes perhaps see the human race navigating in a sea without shoals and in fair weather? No.

They saw Jerusalem falling upon its God; Romans falling upon Jerusalem; Protestantism falling upon the Church; revolutions, nursing at the breasts of Protestantism, falling upon societies; socialists falling upon civilizations; and a terrible and just God falling upon everything. He saw these things. Due to all this, his eyes were filled with tears until the end. And his soul was sad until his death.

Let us now see what he said. What did he say to his disciples?

> Behold I send you as sheep in the midst of wolves. Be ye therefore wise as serpents and simple as doves. But beware of men. For they will deliver you up in councils, and they will scourge you in their synagogues. And you shall be brought before governors, and before kings for my sake, for a testimony to them and to the Gentiles.[3]

Furthermore: "The brother also shall deliver up the brother to death, and the father the son: and the children shall rise up against their parents, and shall put them to death. And you shall be hated by all men for my name's sake: but he that shall persevere unto the end, he shall be saved."[4]

If the destiny of humanity is to be perfect and raise itself up, it is entirely clear that nothing will be more perfect or raised up than at the end of time. So you can now catch a glimpse of what that end will be.

> And it was given unto him to make war with the saints, and to overcome them. And power was given him over every tribe, and people, and tongue, and nation. And all that dwell upon the earth adored him, whose names are not written in the book of life of the Lamb, which was slain from the beginning of the world.[5]
>
> And I saw an angel coming down from heaven, having the key of the bottomless pit, and a great chain in his hand. And he laid hold on the dragon the old serpent, which is the devil and Satan, and bound him for a thousand years. And he cast him into the bottomless pit, and shut him up, and set a seal upon him, that he should no more seduce the nations, till the thousand years be finished. And after that, he must be loosed a little time.[6]

These texts show that the waves of the sea will flood the earth and rise to the heavens above. Few will be saved from that terrible flood. Saints will be vanquished. There will be tribulation, weeping, temptation, and struggle in the flock of the Lord. Finally, everything will succumb if the arm of almighty God does not chain them to monsters.

My doctrine consists in this: the *natural* triumph of evil over good and the *supernatural* triumph of God over evil. Here is the condemnation of all the progressive and perfectionist systems with which modern philosophers, deceivers by profession, have attempted to lull asleep peoples, those immortal infants.

I have not said that we are far from the end. Who can say or know this? What I do know is that this tremendous growth of evil can only come about in two ways: either suddenly and miraculously or progressively and slowly according to the natural law of cause and effect. This first way is impossible because it would result in evil coming from God, not from the freedom of man. Consequently, God would be evil. He would be the Devil, according to Proudhon's blasphemy. If it is impossible to accept the first way, then it is inevitable that the second way be accepted.

Now (and here I really call upon your attention), it is necessary to assume that evil develops itself and grows very old and widespread. Hence it follows that in order for me to show that my observations do not apply to the present era, the impossibility of demonstrating that we are far from the end is not enough. Beyond that, it is necessary to demonstrate what is even more impossible: that we are far from the beginning.

Apart from this, I do not give this last reason except insofar as it is valuable as a subsidiary reason. The last day, next to eternity, is known only by he who is eternal. Aside from this, we are ignorant about everything concerning Heaven and earth.

But it would not be prudent to forget that the human race has already been on a pilgrimage for six thousand years on the earth; that its face, bathed in dust and sweat, is full of gray hair; that this six-thousand-year period is a great Biblical epoch; that Saint Vincent Ferrer[7] was seen as an apocalyptic angel; that the greatest apostasies have consumed Europe; that the light of the Gospel has reached the remotest regions; that many of the prophecies announcing the end have undoubtedly already been fulfilled and that the rest will be fulfilled.

Apart from this and whatever else you think, these two things always happen whenever we take risks: evil always naturally triumphs over good and God always triumphs over evil through an act of his sovereign will. This happened in the era that began with the Creation and ended with the flood. This happened in the era that began with the flood and ended with the arrival of Our Lord Jesus Christ. And it will happen, according to the testimony of the Scriptures, in the era that runs and extends from the coming of Our Lord, as the Savior of man, until his arrival in glory and majesty as the judge of the human race.

Now, there is a law that fulfills itself in everything, always and everywhere. It is a law that appears at the beginning, the middle, and the end of time. It is a divine law that governs the world. It is a law that presides over the development of humanity and shines throughout History. I have not invented it. And I have not seen it. I have done nothing more than demonstrate it and dress it in a formula.

As you see, Catholicism is very far from seeing social and human life through a prism of rich and brilliant colors. Through its eyes it sees life as an expiation and the world as a valley of tears.

What is called evil by man, and what evil is in reality, considering it in its origin, is sin. Sin is converted into good by the hand of God through its effects, whatever they may be, serving as punishment or as expiation. It is always an instrument of God's justice used upon reprobates and of his mercy when applied to saints.

These two points of view—the divine and the human—serve to explain the marvelous contradiction that can be noticed between the judgments and words of Our Lord and the judgments and words of men. "Blessed are they who weep," says the Lord from the mount. And to whom did he say this? He said it to the world, which always mistook his tears as a sign of misfortune. "Blessed are the poor in spirit." He said this to those people and nations always occupied in deifying their pride. The unjustly persecuted were a matter of compassion for the world. But he called then *blessed* before the world. He made them worthy of envy.

The world chose the cross as a symbol of infamy. The Lord chose it as a symbol of victory. The world proclaimed the proud to be great. The Lord proclaimed the humble to be great. The world sanctified pleasures. The Lord sanctified tribulations. For that, at the time of his death, being the absolute Lord of all, he entered into eternity in order to give an inheritance to his most holy mother and to his holy apostles, jewels of a higher value than the cross—tears and martyrdom.

Yes, life is an expiation and the world is a valley of tears. It is useless to rebel against Providence, reason, and History. If you do not want to raise your eyes to Heaven, then set them on the cradle of the child without sin. There, like everywhere else, you will read a terrible lesson. Do you see that child who was born having no will, no understanding, and no strength and who could do nothing, know nothing, or have nothing? In his extreme weakness and ignorance he could only do and know one thing: he could cry and know how to cry. It was only in the shedding of tears that he needed no teacher. *Et nunc intelligite* (And now he understands).

It is said that my opinions are contrary to philosophy and reason. I ask, to what philosophy and to what reason are my opinions opposed? Reason, as it comes from the hand of God, and philosophy, as it comes from its mother, the Catholic religion, are venerable and holy to me. If we mean by reason the faculty that God has given man in order to receive and understand what he reveals and of drawing useful conclusions about life and society from what has been revealed, I respect and venerate human reason as one of God's masterpieces. If reason is the faculty of inventing truth or of discovering, without the help of divine revelation, those fundamental truths that are the mothers of all others, then I do not respect or venerate it. I also resolutely reject it. Its admirers admire a shadow. They actually admire something less than a real shadow. They admire a dreamed shadow. Among the fundamental ideas of all the sciences and of reason there exists the same relationship between exterior objects and the pupils of the eyes. This is not a relationship of *causality*. It is a relationship of *coexistence.*

If by philosophy we mean that science which reduces the fundamental truths of this or that sort revealing a system or method ordering them in a way that forms a harmonious and luminous ensemble, in marking out the relationships in which they are united to others, and in drawing out from its most fruitful breast other secondary truths that can serve in teaching society and man, I respect and venerate it as something honoring and exalting the human race.

This was philosophy in the hands of the Catholic doctors; of Saint Augustine, whom nobody exceeds or equals in sharpness, sagacity, and penetrating genius; of Saint Thomas, who has no competitors in solid, vast, and profound genius. I did not have this class of philosophy in mind when I condemned philosophy in my letters. But if philosophy is considered to be that science of knowing God without God's help, of knowing man without the help of him who formed man, and of knowing society without the help of him who silently rules it; if by philosophy we mean the science that consists in a triple creation—divine, social, and human—I resolutely reject this creation, science, and philosophy. This is precisely what I reject. I reject all rationalist systems that are based upon this absurd principle: that reason is independent of God and competent in everything.

If you ask me about my particular opinion on eclecticism, I will say that it does not exist. It does not exist because, first, if it consists in blindly choosing certain solitary principles from among various philosophical systems, eclecticism would be the innocent recreation of he who, stripping Homeric poems, strips the loose leaves flying about in order to understand the capricious sense of what is fluttering together in the air.

Second, because if it consists in choosing with criteria, philosophy is not in the choice, but in the principle that allows choosing, in which case the unity of criteria, principles, and guidance in the eclectic labyrinth, convert eclecticism into an absolute system. There is still more. Such a choice does not exist because, in the first place, he who begins by assenting to a criterion of choosing does not have the freedom to choose. He is the slave of his criterion.

However, if this is so, then eclecticism can only be considered as a pallid and defoliated branch of the great rationalist tree that brought death into the world. Rationalism came from Spinosaism, Voltairianism, Kantianism, Hegelianism, and Cousinism, all doctrines of perdition that in the political, religious, and social orders is for Europe what the heavenly empire of opium is for the English.

Yes, European society is dying. Its extremities are cold. Its heart will soon stop beating. Do you know why Europe is dying? It is dying because it is poisoned. It is dying because God made it in order to feed itself on Catholic substance, but the empiricist doctors have given it rational substance to eat. It is dying because just as man does not live on bread alone, but on all the words uttered by God, so also societies do not die only by iron, but due to every anti-Catholic word uttered from the mouths of philosophers. It is dying because error kills. And this society is grounded in errors. Everything it holds to be incontestable is false.

The vital strength of truth is so great that if you possess one truth, only one truth, that truth would save you. But its fall is so deep, its decadence so radical, its blindness so complete, its nakedness so absolute, and its misfortune so without precedent that it does not possess a single truth. So, the disaster that must come will be the disaster *par excellence* of History. Individuals can still save themselves because they can always save themselves. But society is lost. And this is so not because it seems to me that it cannot save itself. There is no salvation for society because we do not want our sons to be Christian and because we are not true Christians. Society cannot be saved because the Catholic spirit, the only spirit of life, no longer gives anything life. It does not give life to education, governments, institutions, laws, or customs.

I am aware that changing the course of things, in the state they are in today, would be an enterprise fit for giants. There is no power in the world that can accomplish this by itself. And such an enterprise could not be brought to a happy end even if one power was to work in cooperation with all others. I leave it to your care to investigate if this cooperation is possible, to what extent it is possible, and to decide if, even if it is possible in this case, if the salvation of society would not completely be a miracle.

It is already time to end this letter, which robs you of the space you need in order to air other matters. In conclusion, allow me to make an important observation. Of all the powers born from the new organization of European societies, none is as large and exorbitant as the power conceded to those who impose their word of hatred upon the people. Modern societies have conferred upon everyone the power to be journalists. The tremendous task of teaching the people that Jesus Christ entrusted to his apostles has been given to journalists.

I do not want to pass judgment upon this institution right now. I shall only point out your greatness to you. Your profession is a civil priesthood as well as a militia. The instrument that you manage can be for salvation or for death. The word is sharper than the sword, faster than a ray of light, and more destructive than war.

You ministers of the social word, never forget that the most terrible responsibility always accompanies this terrible ministry; that there is not enough punishment in eternity, in the bosom of Abraham, in order to castigate those who place the word, that divine word, in the service of error, just as there are not enough rewards for those who consecrate their words and talents to the service of God and man.

Be assured of my best wishes. Please be honored to accept the greetings of your friend and servant.

—Juan Donoso Cortés

NOTES

1. *El Pais* and *El Heraldo* were the leading liberal publications in Spain in the nineteenth century.
2. John 1: 11–13.
3. Matthew 10: 16–18.
4. Matthew 10: 21–22.
5. Apocalypse 13: 7–8.
6. Apocalypse 20: 1–3.
7. Vincent Ferrer was a Spaniard and brother of the Dominican order. Due to a vision he claimed to have in 1396, he led a penitential group of flagellants through Spain, France, and Italy.

Speech on the Situation in Europe

Having retired from the political scene for reasons that are known by my friends and imagined by everyone else, I had not planned to take part in this or any other discussion today.[1] If I break this silence today, it is in order to fulfill a duty, a duty that I esteem sacred, as I esteem sacred all my duties. My sad prognoses previously concerned Europe in general. Today, unfortunately, they also concern the Spanish nation. I believe, gentlemen, I believe with the deepest conviction, that we have entered a distressing period. All the symptoms that announce it come together at the same time: blindness in understanding, inflamed spirits, aimless discussions, wars without reason. Mainly, and most importantly, and what is missed most by the Congress, is the furor that has seized everyone over economic reforms. This furor that raises so many questions never presents itself as the most important of all without it being a sure announcement of great catastrophe and ruin.

Gentlemen, entrusted by the Commission with the task of summarizing this long, important, and sad debate, I will be, however, relatively brief for several reasons because the question has been placed in my hands already exhausted; because I am not here in order to speak nor is the Congress here in order to hear me; and because, disregarding the dramatic episodes, terribly dramatic, disregarding the personal allusions, the attacks directed at the ministers, which the ministers have answered, and finally disregarding oratorical displays, there remain three or four arguments that need to be summarized. In this discussion, gentlemen, there have been sometimes scathing and harsh words. I will be neither harsh nor scathing.

May Heaven permit, gentlemen, that before entering on such a perditious course my tongue may stick to my palate and that my voice may drown in my throat. Mr. San Miguel[2] has told us that he was not in favor of tactics that place men in opposition with themselves, with others in the same party, and with their parties. I also will not adopt this tactic. I will not speak about those things which I, on my part, do not give any importance. How will I ignore that there are differences, in special cases, between men of the same party, when since I was born I have been looking for one man who is in agreement with himself? I still have not found one.

Gentlemen, human nature is inharmonious, antithetical, and contradictory. Man is condemned to take to his grave the chain of all his contradictions. Also, I will not speak about the changes and movements of the parties. However, gentlemen, how can we ignore the changes and movements of the parties? Is not life, human life, like that of the universe, in perpetual transformation? What is youth if it is not a transformation of childhood? Is age nothing other than the transformation of youth? And what is death, for a Christian, if it is not a transformation of life?

Gentlemen, now I will deal with the main arguments, and nothing else, with the greatest brevity that is possible for me. The first question that I am going to discuss concerns the constitutionality of the budget authorizations. This is the question that all the speakers have addressed, whether they supported or opposed them. In this matter there are two theories, and no more than two. According to one theory, discussion is a right. Being a right, it can be renounced whenever it seems convenient and opportune. This is the monarchic theory. There is another theory that is democratic. It consists in the notion that "All discussion is an obligation; it is a duty," as Mr. San Miguel says. Being an obligation, a duty, it cannot be renounced.

But the arguments used here against the constitutionality of the budget authorizations are neither monarchic nor democratic. They are not arguments at all. The gentlemen in these benches, as well as in the other benches, have attacked the principle of authorization, and have concluded by saying: "Discussion is obligatory for the deputies." And then they say: "But discussions about budget authorizations are only licit in some situations."

This is a contradiction. And so that this can be seen, we will reduce these theories to three syllogisms. The monarchic syllogism: Rights can be renounced, and they are things that can be renounced by their nature. This is how discussion is a right of the Congress. Then the Congress can renounce it whenever it so desires. The democratic syllogism: discussion in the Congress is an obligation. Here obligations are not renounced. Therefore, the Congress can never renounce them. I understand monarchy and democracy. I do not understand what either the one or the other is not.

Let us see now the syllogism that combines both of these positions. It will be seen, as it is presented, what is lacking in its connection. It is the following: discussion is an obligation. Therefore, obligations cannot be renounced. But sometimes they can be renounced. This is the syllogism combining the opposing positions. And what does it want to say? It wants to say that the opposing positions reject monarchy with their premises while rejecting democracy with their conclusions. They are a perpetual rejection, and they are condemned to sterility, like all rejections.

But it has been said: "Even though discussions about authorizations were permitted concerning other matters, they cannot be, nor should they be, permitted in the question of budgets." And why, gentlemen? I conceive this argument from the perspective of a certain school. This school holds that assemblies have not been established only in order to discuss budgets and that budgets are established only in order to be discussed in assemblies. But those who support constitutional monarchy, as it is found among us and in the rest of Europe, must recognize that the deputies of the nation, who come here to debate and vote, have the same right to discuss all the laws that are presented here, whether they concern budgets, politics, economics, and even, to a certain extent, religion. Consequently, since a right is the same thing as an obligation, some of the same principles should be applied in discussing everything.

One of the gentlemen seated in those benches asked a question that still has not been answered in the way that it was posed. He asked, "If these debates do not cease, the budget will never be discussed. Is there here any deputy who dares to say that they should not be discussed?" I shall deal with this question by giving this reply. But first I need to say something else. The gentleman deputy to whom I allude tells us, with statistics in hand, that here the discussion of budgets would have lasted ordinarily five or six months.

Very well, assuming this, I ask the following question. Does the Cortes have the right to discuss other laws that do not concern budgets? Yes or no? If you tell me that it does not have the right to discuss other laws, I will say: Then leave this institution. For you fall into a semiabsolutist and semidemocratic school, born in our days, which concentrates all the powers of society in one place by granting a single man the title of president of the Council of Ministers. These powers are absolute. Tyranny is located in this man and, at the same time, democracy is located in an Assembly that has no power, except that of stabbing the tyrant to death by denying him subsidies. This is the semiabsolutist and semidemocratic theory that was recently born in the French Republic.

So, gentlemen, if I am told, on the contrary, that the Cortes is entitled to discuss all laws, as it is entitled to discuss budgets, then I will ask another question. Do the gentlemen deputies believe that the Cortes should be permanent or that its sessions should be intermittent? If I am told that the Cortes should be permanent, I respond: You depart from the spirit of our institutions, because a constitutional Cortes is never permanent. A republican Cortes is permanent. Do you say that it should not be permanent? Do you say that it should be intermittent? Then you want what is impossible, because a discussion about budgets that lasts only six months is impossible. And, beside this discussion come other discussions that are of interest to the State. Consequently, you place yourselves between two reefs. So, after asking a question, I respond now to the question that I have posed. Yes, the Cortes should discuss budgets, but it should not discuss them in whatever form it desires.

But now I proceed, gentlemen, to the great question, because in all the matters that are aired in Congresses, and anywhere else, there are many questions. But only one is true, and I go to the true question. The true question is the economic question, considered politically. Thus considered, I must refute three serious errors which have been committed by everyone: the progressive opposition, the conservative opposition, the Ministry, to a certain extent, and also, to a certain extent, public opinion.

Gentlemen, I attack error wherever I find it; and I will attack it where I have found it. Let us look at the three positions that I have characterized as errors, and that I refute. First error: Economic questions are, in themselves, the most important ones. Second error: The time has arrived in Spain that these questions be given the importance that indeed they have. Third error: Economic reforms are not only possible, but simple. These three errors have been incurred by all sides. I have risen only in order to refute everyone in this land, in order to refute these errors.

The authority of statesmen has been used here to support the first of these three propositions. If we speak of statesmen, as they are now considered, I do not deny that authority. However, if we are referring to those men of colossal stature who are considered founders of empires, civilizers of nations, who have received a providential responsibility with diverse titles, in diverse times, and with diverse ends; if we are speaking about those immortal men, who are the patrimony and the glory of human generations, I deny it. If we are only referring to that magnificent dynasty, which begins with Moses, goes through Charlemagne, and ends with Napoleon, I deny it. If it is those immortal men, I deny it absolutely.

No man who has ever attained immortality has found his glory in economic truth. All such men have founded nations on the foundations of social and religious truths. I am not saying (because I foresee the arguments and want to deal with them before they arise) that I believe governments are supposed to neglect economic questions.

I do not believe that nations should be badly administered. Gentlemen, am I so lacking in reason, so lacking in heart, that I could go so far astray? I am saying no such thing. But I do say that each question has its proper place. And the place for these questions is in the third or fourth place, not the first. That is what I am saying.

It has been said that bringing up these questions here was the means of defeating socialism. Ah, gentlemen, the means of defeating socialism! But, what is socialism if not an economic sect? Socialism is the child of political economy like a small viper is the child of a snake. The viper devours its own mother right after it is born.

Entertain these economic questions, put them in the first place, and I will tell you that within two years you will have to contend with all the socialist questions in the Parliament as well as in the streets. Do you want to fight socialism? You cannot fight it this way. And this opinion, before strong spirits have laughed, already causes no laughter either in Europe or in the world. If you want to combat socialism, it is necessary that you go to that religion which teaches the poor to be resigned and the rich to be merciful.Gentlemen, I now proceed to the second error, which claims that the day already has arrived when these questions can be treated with the importance that indeed they have.

Gentlemen, this idea was born last summer. The social revolution was defeated in the streets of Madrid,[3] the dynastic question was resolved in Catalan fields,[4] public opinion was blind then because it is almost always blind. Being blind in this matter, because it is always blind, public opinion held that we were so sure about life that we could look after finances exclusively.

What a huge mistake. However, then the error was excusable. Today it is not excused either by public opinion, by the Government, or by the conservative opposition. Today, who would dare to say that we are secure? Who does not see the clouds on the dark horizon?

Now then, if we are so hesitant today, how is it possible that yesterday we were so firm? And if yesterday we were firm, why are we so hesitant today? Gentlemen, I will tell you the truth. The truth is that we are not so firm today, because we were not firm yesterday. And we were not firm yesterday, because we have never been firm since the February Revolution. Since that most memorable revolution, nothing is firm, nothing is secure in Europe. Spain is firmer, gentlemen, and you already see what it is. This Congress is the best, and you already see what it is. Gentlemen, Spain is to Europe what an oasis is in the desert of the Sahara.

I have conversed with the sages, and I know how little wisdom is valued in these circumstances. I have conversed with the brave, and I know how little courage is valued in these circumstances. I have conversed with the most prudent of men, and I know how thin prudence is in these moments. Gentlemen, look at the state of Europe. No statesmen appear except when they have lost the gift of counsel.

Human reason suffers eclipses. Institutions sway and great nations become suddenly decadent. Gentlemen, look with me at Europe from Poland to Portugal. Tell me, with a hand placed over the heart, tell me in good faith if you find a single society that can say: I am firm in my foundations. Tell me if you find a single foundation that can say: I am firm within myself.

And I say myself, gentlemen, that the revolution has been defeated in Spain; that it has been defeated in Italy; that it has been defeated in France; and that it has been defeated in Hungary. However, gentlemen, this is not the truth. The truth is that with the most supreme concentration of social forces, even the most extreme of those forces, it has hardly been enough, and they have not even barely done enough, in order to contain the monster.

From here the progress of socialism is not known, except in France. However, it is known that socialism has three large theaters. Its disciples are in France, and nothing but its disciples. Its thrones[5] are in Italy, and nothing but its thrones. Its pontiffs and teachers are in Germany.[6]

Gentlemen, the truth is that, in spite of these victories, there have been no victories, except in name. The frightening sphinx is before your eyes, and there is not a single Œdipus who knows how to decipher the enigma. The truth is that a tremendous problem lies before us, and Europe does not know how to resolve it. This is the truth.

To the man who possesses good reason, good sense, and penetrating genius, everything points to a near and fateful crisis. Everything announces a cataclysm that has never before been seen by men. And if not, gentlemen, think about those symptoms that never appear, and that rarely appear together, without being followed by fearful catastrophes. Today they lead to perdition. Some are lost by surrendering, while others are lost by resisting.

There are ambitious princes where weakness is the cause of death. Gentlemen, God places knowledgeable princes where talent itself is supposed to be the cause of perdition.

And what happens to princes also happens to ideas. All ideas, the most disgusting as well as the most magnificent, produce the same results. And if not, gentlemen, cast your eyes upon Paris and Venice and see the result of the demagogic as well as magnificent idea of Italian independence. What happens to princes and to ideas also happens to men.

Gentlemen, where a single man would suffice in order to save society, this man does not exist. And if he does exist, God disperses a little poison in the winds for him. On the contrary, when a single man could lose society, that man comes forward, is supported strongly by the people, and finds level roads. If you want to see the contrast, gentlemen, cast your eyes upon the tomb of Marshall Bugeaud[7] and upon the throne of Mazzini.[8] What happens to princes, ideas, and men also happens to parties.

And here, gentlemen, because this is more immediately applicable to us, I call upon your attention. Where the salvation of society consists in the dissolution of all the old parties and in the formation of one new party, made up of all the others, there, gentlemen, the parties insist on not being dissolved, and are not dissolved. That is what would happen in France. The salvation of France, gentlemen, would be brought about by the breakup of the Bonapartist party, the legitimist party, and the Orleanist party[9] and the formation of a single monarchist party.

However, where the dissolution of the parties produces the salvation of society, the Bonapartists think of Bonaparte, the Orleanists of the Count of Paris, the legitimists of Henry V. And on the contrary, wherever the salvation of society would consist in the parties conserving their old banners, which they do not tear from their breasts, because all their followers could fight together in large and noble contests, wherever this is necessary for the salvation of society, like here in Spain, gentlemen, the parties are dissolved.

Gentlemen, economic reform is not the essential remedy for this evil. The fall of a government and its replacement by another government is not a remedy. The fundamental error in this matter consists in believing that the evils Europe suffers are born of governments. I cannot deny the influence of government on the governed. How can this be denied? Who could ever deny this? But the evil is much deeper than this; it is much more serious. Evil is not in governments. It is in the governed. The evil is in how the governed have become ungovernable.

Gentlemen, the true cause of the deep and profound evil that troubles Europe is in how the notion of divine and human authority has disappeared. This is the evil troubling Europe; this is the evil troubling society; this is the evil troubling the world. And this is why, gentlemen, nations are ungovernable. This explains a phenomenon that I have not heard explained by anyone, and that has, however, a satisfactory explanation.

All who have traveled throughout France agree in saying that they have not encountered one Frenchman who is a republican. I myself can give testimony to the truth of this because I have traveled throughout France. But you may wonder: If there are no republicans in France then how can the Republic subsist? No one has given the reason for this. But I will give it. The Republic subsists in France, and I say more, the Republic will subsist in France, because the Republic is the necessary form of government for a nation that is ungovernable.

Among ungovernable peoples, the form of government is necessarily republican. This is why the Republic subsists, and will subsist, in France. It matters little that it is opposed by the will of men or that it is sustained by force. This explains the duration of the French Republic.

Upon hearing me speak at the same time about divine and human authority, someone will ask me what political questions have to do with religious questions? Gentlemen, I do not know if there is any deputy here who does not believe there is a relationship between religious matters and politics. But if there is, I am going to demonstrate their necessary relationship in such a way that he will be able to see it with his own eyes and touch it with his own hands.

Gentlemen, civilization has two phases, one that I will call affirmative, because in it civilization rests upon affirmations; I will also call it progressive because those affirmations, upon which civilization rests, are truths; and, finally, I will call it Catholic, because Catholicism is that which fully embraces all these truths and affirmations.[10] And there is another phase of civilization that I will call negative, because it rests exclusively upon denials. I will also call it decadent, because these denials are errors; and I will call it revolutionary, because these errors finally are converted into revolutions that transform States.

Very well, gentlemen, what are the three affirmations of this civilization that I call affirmative, progressive, and Catholic? These three religious affirmations assert that a personal God exists. These are three affirmations. First, an omnipresent personal God exists. Second, a personal God, that is everywhere, reigns in Heaven and upon the earth. Third, this God, that reigns in Heaven and upon the earth, absolutely governs divine and human things.

Now, gentlemen, since there are these three affirmations in the religious order, there are also three other affirmations in the political order. There is a king who is everywhere present by means of his agents. This omnipresent king reigns over his subjects. And this king, who reigns over his subjects, governs his subjects. So, the political affirmations are nothing more than the consequences of the religious affirmations. There are two kinds of political institutions symbolizing these three affirmations: absolute monarchies and constitutional monarchies. This is how moderates of all countries understand them, because no moderate party has ever rejected a king, or his existence, or his reign, or his government. Consequently, constitutional monarchy enters with the same title as absolute monarchy by symbolizing the three political affirmations, that are the echo, if we may say so, of the three religious affirmations.

Gentlemen, the period of the civilization upon which these three affirmations rest—a period that I have called affirmative, progressive, and Catholic—has ended. Now we are entering, gentlemen, the second period, that which I have called negative and revolutionary. In this second period there are three denials, corresponding to the first three affirmations.

The first denial, or as I will call it, the denial of the first degree in the religious order, is that God exists and reigns. But God is so high, that he cannot govern human affairs. This is the first denial, the first degree of denial, in this negative period of civilization. And what does this denial, concerning the providence of God, correspond to in the political order? In the political order the progressive party does not respond to the deist, who denies Providence. Rather, it says: "The king exists, the king reigns; but he does not govern." So, gentlemen, a progressive constitutional monarchy belongs to the first degree of negative civilization.

Second denial: The deist denies Providence. Those who favor constitutional monarchy, as progressives understand it, deny government. However, in the religious order, the pantheist comes along and says: "God exists, but God does not have a personal existence. God is not a person, and since he is not a person, he neither governs nor reigns. God is all that we see. He is neither everything that lives nor everything that moves. God is humanity." This is what the pantheist says. Since the pantheist denies the personal existence of God, although not his absolute existence, he also denies God's reign and Providence.

Immediately, gentlemen, the republican comes along and says, "Power exists, but power is not personal and neither reigns nor governs. Power is all that lives, all that exists, all that moves. Therefore, it is with the masses. So, there is no other means of government than universal suffrage. And there is no government other than a republic."

So, gentlemen, pantheism in the religious order corresponds to the republicanism in the political order. There is a further and last denial. And there can be no denial beyond this point. After the deist and the pantheist comes the atheist who says: "God neither reigns nor governs and is neither a person nor a crowd. God does not exist." Gentlemen, based upon this, Proudhon says, "there is no government." So, gentlemen, one denial calls out to another denial, just as an abyss calls out to another abyss. Beyond that denial, which is the abyss, there is nothing but darkness, a palpable darkness.

Now then, gentlemen, what is the state of Europe? Europe is entering into the second denial, and is heading toward the third, which is the last. Do not forget this. If you desire something more concrete on the dangers afflicting societies, I will be more concrete, although with a certain prudence. Everyone is aware of my official position. I cannot speak about Europe without speaking about Germany. I cannot speak about Germany without speaking about Prussia, which represents Germany. I cannot speak about Prussia without speaking about its king, gentlemen, about whom it is said in passing, due to his eminent qualities, can be called an eminent German,. The Congress will notgive the certain reserve I maintain while bringing up this question which concerns Europe. With regard to Prussia, one must maintain an almost absolute reserve. But I will say, however, that will suffice in order to manifest my concrete ideas on the specific dangers also threatening Europe.

Gentlemen, the danger posed to Europe by Russia has been discussed here. And for the time being, and beyond, I believe that I can reassure the Congress that there is no greater danger that one can fear than Russia. Gentlemen, the influence that Russia exercised in Europe was exercised through the German Confederation. The German Confederation was made against Paris, the revolutionary city, the damned city, and in favor of Petersburg, the city of restored traditions. What resulted from this? The Confederation was not an empire since it could not be one. It was not an empire because Russia could never accommodate a German empire nor a reunification of the entire German race by its side. So the Confederation was composed of microscopic principalities and two great monarchies. What do you suppose led to the war with France? It suited Russia that these were absolute monarchies. And these two monarchies were absolute. See here, gentlemen, how it happened that the influence of Russia, since the time of the German Confederation until the February Revolution, extended from Petersburg to Paris.

But, gentlemen, since the February Revolution everything has moved in a similar way. The revolutionary hurricane has overthrown thrones, pulverized crowns, and humiliated kings. The German Confederation does not exist. Today chaos reigns in Germany. Gentlemen, it can be said that the influence of Russia, that extended, as I said, from Petersburg to Paris, has now been succeeded by the demagogic influence of Paris, which extends as far as Poland.

Here is the difference. Russia had two powerful allies: Austria and Prussia. Today it is known that it no longer can count on Austria. But Austria must unceasingly struggle against the demagogic spirit that exists there as it does everywhere, and against the racial spirit that exists there more than anywhere else. And finally, it must reserve all its forces for a possible struggle with Prussia. So, gentlemen, with Austria neutralized, and not being able to count upon the German Confederation, Russia cannot count upon its own forces for more than a day. And does the Congress know how large are the forces Russia has at its disposal for offensive purposes? They have never been more than 300,000 men. And does the Congress know with whom those 300,000 men must fight? They must fight all the German races, represented by Prussia. They must fight all the Latin races, represented by France. They must fight the most noble and powerful Anglo-Saxon race, represented by England. Such a conflict, gentlemen, would be senseless; it would be absurd on the part of Russia. In the case of a general war, the sure result, most certainly, would be that Russia would no longer be a European power. It would be nothing more than an Asian power. This is why Russia avoids war; and this is why England wants war.

Gentlemen, war would have exploded if it had not been for the chronic weakness of France, which did not want to continue on this course with England, for Austrian prudence, and for the most wise prudence of Russian diplomacy. For this reason, gentlemen, because Russia has not wanted it, because it could not have wanted it, war has not broken out over the question of the Turkish refugees.[11] However, do not believe that for this reason I hold the opinion that Europe has nothing to fear from Russia. I believe quite the contrary. But I also believe that if Russia is to take possession of Europe, three things are necessary before that can happen, all of which, as can be seen, gentlemen, is not only possible, but also probable.

First, it is necessary that after the revolution has dissolved society, it would also dissolve the permanent armies. Second, when socialism despoils property owners it extinguishes patriotism, because a robbed property owner is not a patriot, nor can he be one. When the question comes framed in this supreme and anguished way, there is no patriotism in man. Third, the end will come when the attempt is made to form a powerful confederation of all the Slavic peoples under the influence and protection of Russia. The Slavic nations have, gentlemen, eighty million inhabitants.

Now then, when there are no permanent armies in Europe, having been dissolved by revolution; when there is no patriotism in Europe, having been extinguished by socialist revolutions; when the great confederation of the Slavic peoples has been established in Eastern Europe; when there are no more than two large armies in the West, the army of the despoilers and the army of the despoiled, then, gentlemen, the time will have come for Russia. Then Russia will be able to stroll calmly, fully armed, all the way to our country. And then, gentlemen, the world will witness the greatest punishment ever in the memory of History.

Gentlemen, that tremendous punishment will be the punishment of England. England's ships will be no defense against the colossal Empire that will embrace Europe with one arm and India with the other. Nothing will save England: its colossal Empire will fall prostrate, broken into pieces, and its dismal death-rattle and its penetrating groan will resonate to the ends of the earth.

Gentlemen, do not believe that the catastrophes will end there. The Slavic races are not to the peoples of West what the German races were to the Romans. No, the Slavic races have been in contact with civilization for some time. They are semi-civilized races. The Russian administration is the most corrupt of all. Now then, gentlemen, with Russia placed in the midst of a conquered Europe lying prostrate at its feet, it will absorb into its veins the civilization it has drunk and killed. Russia will not delay falling into corruption. Then, gentlemen, I do not know what will be the universal cautery that God has prepared for that desperate universal multitude.

Against this, gentlemen, there is only one remedy, and only one: the bond of the future is England. In the first place, gentlemen, the Anglo-Saxon race is the most generous, the most noble, and the most powerful in the world. In the second place, the Anglo-Saxon race is the one that is least exposed to the impulse of revolutions. I believe it is easier for there to be a revolution in Saint Petersburg than in London. What does England need in order to impede the inevitable conquest of all Europe by Russia? What does it need?

It needs to avoid what it would lose: the breakup of its permanent armies through revolution. It needs to avoid the plunder of Europe through socialism. Furthermore, gentlemen, England needs a foreign policy that is monarchic and conservative. But that would be nothing more than a palliative. A monarchic and conservative England could impede the dissolution of European society up to a certain point and only for a certain time. This is so because England is not powerful enough, it is not strong enough, in order to nullify the dissolvent force of the doctrines spread throughout the world. But this nullification is necessary.

In order for the palliative to become a remedy, it would be necessary, gentlemen, that England, besides being conservative and monarchic, also be Catholic. Gentlemen, I maintain there is no other remedy than Catholicism, because Catholicism is the only doctrine that is the absolute contradiction of socialism. Gentlemen, what is Catholicism? It is wisdom and humility. What is socialism, gentlemen? It is pride and barbarism. Socialism, gentlemen, is a king and a beast at the same time.

Gentlemen, the Congress may have missed the fact that while I have been speaking about the dangers threatening society and the world, I have not spoken about the French nation. Gentlemen, there is a reason for this. Until recently France was a great nation. Nowadays, gentlemen, it is not even a nation; it is the central club of Europe.

So, gentlemen, it has been shown: First, that economic questions are not, should not, and cannot be the most important of all. Second, that state of peacefulness and security, which would allow us to dedicate ourselves to those questions exclusively, has not arrived. Now, gentlemen, I shall proceed to refute the third and last error, which maintains that economies are not only possible, but simple.

Gentlemen, the Congress will permit me now, like before, to tell the truth, only the truth, and the whole truth, with the frankness and good faith that characterize me. No deputy could possibly doubt this axiom: Governments, even those offering the greatest advantages, produce some inconveniences in return for their advantages. And on the contrary, even those governments producing the greatest disadvantages also offer some advantages in return for those same disadvantages. And, lastly, there are no immortal governments.

In this place I can speak in complete freedom about the advantages and the disadvantages and even the death of governments, because all of them have their disadvantages and their advantages. And all of them perish. Therefore, gentlemen, I say that in return for the serious disadvantages that absolute governments produce, they have one great advantage. They are relatively cheap. And I say that, in return for the great advantages that constitutional governments have, they have one serious disadvantage. They are expensive. I do not know of any more expensive form of government than a republican government. Arguing by analogy, it is easy to foresee the fortune of each one of these governments. I say, gentlemen, that the most probable thing is that all absolute governments, wherever they exist, perish through discussion. All constitutional governments, wherever they exist, perish through bankruptcy. This is my intimate conviction, gentlemen. I make the gentlemen deputies repositories of my convictions.

There is only one way, gentlemen, of carrying out reforms, especially great economic reforms. That single means is by disbanding, or partially disbanding, permanent armies. This, gentlemen, could liberate governments from bankruptcy for some time. But that disbanding would be the complete ruin of society. Gentlemen, I wish to call your attention to this point: Permanent armies are today the only things that impede the fall of civilization into barbarism. Nowadays, gentlemen, we have witnessed a new spectacle in History and in the world. When, gentlemen, when has it ever been seen in the world, except today, that civilization is maintained by weapons and barbarism by ideas? This is what we are seeing in the world at the very hour in which I am speaking.

This phenomenon, gentlemen, is so serious, it is so strange, that it demands an explanation by me. All true civilization comes from Christianity. It is certain that all civilization has been concentrated within the Christian zone. Outside of that zone there is no civilization; everything is barbarian. And, it is certain that before Christianity there had been no civilized nation in the world, not a single one. Not one, gentlemen. I say that there had been no civilized peoples. The Romans and the Greeks were no different. They were cultured peoples. But that is something very different. Culture is the varnish, and nothing more than the varnish, of civilizations. Christianity civilizes the world in three ways: It has civilized the world by making authority inviolable, by making obedience something sacred, and by making self-denial and sacrifice, or, to say it better, charity, something divine. This is how Christianity has civilized nations. Now then (and here is the solution to that great problem), the ideas concerning the inviolability of authority, sanctity, obedience, and the divinity of sacrifice are not found in civil society today. They are found in the temples where the just and merciful

God is adored, and in the camps where the strong God, the God of battles, is adored under the symbols of glory. For this reason, only the Church and the military conserve completely the notions of the inviolability of authority, the sanctity of obedience, and the divinity of charity. For this reason they are today the two representatives of European civilization.

I do not know, gentlemen, if your attention has been called, like mine has been, to the similarity, to the quasi-identity between two people who seem more different and more contrary. I am referring to the likeness between the priest and the soldier. Neither the one nor the other lives for himself; neither the one nor the other lives for his family. For both of them, glory is in sacrifice and self-denial. The responsibility of the soldier is to safeguard the independence of civil society. The responsibility of the priest is to safeguard the independence of religious society. The duty of the priest is to die, to give his life, like a good shepherd, for his sheep. The duty of the soldier, like a good brother, is to give his life for his brethren. If you consider the harshness of the priestly life, you will find that the priesthood, the real priesthood, is a true military. If you consider the sanctity of the military ministry, you will almost find the military to be a true priesthood. What would become of the world, what would become of civilization, what would become of Europe if there were neither priests nor soldiers?

And in view of this, gentlemen, if there is anyone who believes, after what I have just explained, that armies should be disbanded, let him arise and say so. If there is no one, gentlemen, then I must laugh at all your economies, because all your economies are utopias. Do you know what you are attempting when you try to save society with your economies without disbanding the army? You are attempting to put out the fire in the nation with a glass of water. This is what you attempt. I have shown now, as I proposed to show, that economic questions are not the most important. I have also shown that the occasion has not arrived when we can deal with them exclusively; that economic reforms are not simple and, to a certain extent, they are not possible.

Now, gentlemen, there are some speakers who have said to the Congress that by voting for the budget authorization one is voting against representative government. I will turn to those deputies and ask them: Do you want to vote for representative government? Then vote for the budget authorization that is requested by the Government. Vote for it, because if representative governments live upon wise discussions, they die through endless discussions. A great example of this, gentlemen, is Germany, if experience and examples are of any use. Germany has had three constituent assemblies at the same time: one in Vienna, another in Berlin, and another in Frankfurt. The first assembly died by means of an imperial order. A royal order killed the second one. And as for the Assembly of Frankfurt, that Assembly made up of the most eminent sages, of the greatest patricians, of the profoundest philosophers, what happened to it? What happened to that Assembly? The world has never seen such an august senate and a more lamentable end. A universal acclamation gave it life; and universal heckling condemned it to death.

Germany, gentlemen, raised up that Assembly like a divinity in a temple. And that same Germany allowed it to die like a prostitute in a tavern. Gentlemen, that is the history of the German assemblies. And do you know why they died in such a way? I will tell you. They died in this way because they were not allowed to govern. And they did not govern. They died in this way because after more than one year of discussion, nothing was left after their endless discussions, except smoke. Gentlemen, they aspired to the dignity of queens. But God made them sterile, and removed the dignity of motherhood.

Deputies of the nation, look well at the life of the Spanish assemblies! And you, gentlemen of the conservative opposition, I ask you also to look at your future; look, gentlemen, at the future of your party. We have always fought together. We still fight together. Your divisiveness is sacrilegious. The Fatherland will call you to give an account of yourselves on the day of its great misfortune. That day may not be far off. He who does not see that as possible suffers an incurable blindness. If you are belligerent, if you want to fight here, keep your weapons for that day. Do not precipitate conflicts. Gentlemen, is it not enough that every hour has its pain, every day its anguish, and every month its work? When that day of tribulation arrives, there will be so much anguish that we will call even our political opponents brethren. Then you will be sorry, although it will be too late, in having labeled as enemies those who are your brethren.

NOTES

1. This speech was delivered before the Spanish parliament, the Cortes, on 30 January 1850. It concerned the proposed budget authorizations for the Spanish government for that year. It caused a major controversy throughout Europe. The speech was published in Spain and was also translated and published in French, German, Italian, and English. The French conservative and Ultramontanist paper *L'Univers* of Louis Veuillot, a close friend and ideological ally of Donoso, disseminated fourteen thousand copies of the speech. The speech was highly praised by Metternich. The exiled Russian anarchist, Alexander Herzen, agreed with many aspects of the speech and published his own critique of it. However, Herzen was highly critical of Donoso's claim that religions, armies, soldiers, and priests were the last and best defenses of European civilization against the victory of barbarism, socialism, and Russia. See John T. Graham, *Donoso Cortés: Utopian Romanticist and Political Realist* (Columbia: University of Missouri Press, 1974), pp. 151–160.

2. General Evaristo San Miguel (1785–1862), prominent leader of the right wing of the Progressive Party and founding member of the Liberal Union in 1856.

3. This is a reference to the bloody riots that occurred in Madrid in 1834.

4. This is a reference to the First Carlist War (1833–1840). See Edgar Holt, *The Carlist Wars in Spain* (Chester Springs: Dufour Editions, 1967).

5. This refers to the Sardinian monarchy, which sided with the revolutionary forces seeking to unify Italy.

6. This is probably a reference to Karl Marx and Friedrich Engels who published their influential *Communist Manifesto* in 1848.

7. Marshall Thomas-Robert Bugeaud de Piconerie, Duke of Isly, (1784–1849) was the governor of French Algeria in 1840. He consolidated the French hold on Algeria and led the French forces that conquered Morocco for France. As a prominent conservative he led the French army against the February Revolution in 1848.

8. Giuseppe Mazzini (1805–1872) was one of the principal revolutionary leaders and architects of Italian unity. Donoso had little sympathy with his republican ideas, which inspired the revolution in Italy in 1848.

9. The Bonapartists sought to restore the Empire under the rule of a member of the family of Napoleon Bonaparte; the legitimists supported the restoration of the Bourbon

monarchy; the Orleanists supported the establishment of a monarchy under Orleans branch of the French royal family.

10. This is a further development of the theme of the two civilizations in the *Letters to the Count of Montalembert.* The theme is more fully developed in the *Ensayo sobre el catolicismo, el liberalismo y el socialismo*, Bk. I.

11. This is a reference to the problems that led to the Crimean War (1853–1856) in which Great Britain, France, and Turkey were allied against Russia.

Letter to Queen María Cristina

Madam:

The free and generous liberty that Your Majesty[1] has always given to those who have the pleasure of being around you, especially to me, gives me the boldness necessary to submit to Your Majesty's prudent consideration some observations on recent events that will greatly influence the future of the Spanish nation.

The joyous day when Her Majesty[2] is to give birth is drawing near. This will be a happy day for everyone, for our own people as well as for others, because one of the greatest monarchies in Europe will have an heir on that day. In all circumstances and times this has been a happy event. Today when every monarchy seems ready to fall, when the most stable and powerful ones have either fallen or fear falling before the momentum of hurricanes, this birth will be a most happy and memorable event.

Newspapers in the capital have already announced some of the great celebrations that will mark the occasion. Since nothing seems more natural nor more in keeping with ancient customs than the celebration of such a happy event with festivals and merriment, I hope that Your Majesty will permit me, nevertheless, to observe that the diversity of the times in which we live requires a certain analogous diversity in customs. Also, these times do not permit us to follow the customs of our forefathers without any sort of change. Our forefathers lived in peaceful times for nations. Those times were also splendid and great for monarchies. We live in times of such desolation and anguish that one cannot say whether or not all the monarchies and nations shall be shipwrecked.

By writing to Your Majesty, it is not my intention to write a dissertation about what has so lamentably become of Europe. I will limit myself only to recording here one notorious fact. Europe is not afflicted with a variety of different illnesses. It is afflicted with only one illness that is a contagious epidemic.

Everywhere the result is the same since it has manifested the same set of symptoms in every case. The only difference between some nations is that a few of them are still in the invasion stage, while others are in the last stage of illness. Some suffer from a sickness that leads to death, while others are actually dying. This is the state of Europe.

To believe that the inclination to revolt afflicts all peoples as well as all the needy classes is a phenomenon that does not have the same general cause, will seem to Your Majesty, as it seems to me, to be extravagant and insane. There have always been poor as well as rich people in the world. Madam, today the needy classes do not rise up against the comfortable classes unless the comfortable lack charity towards the needy. If the rich had not lost the virtue of charity, God would not have permitted the loss of patience among the poor. The simultaneous loss of these two Christian virtues explains the great fluctuations within societies as well as the turmoil endured throughout the world.

Patience will not return to the hearts of the poor if charity does not return to the hearts of the rich. Madam, today this is the most imperative of all social necessities. To accomplish this, or to contribute to what can accomplish this, must be today the proper office and august responsibility of kings and queens. I am fully aware that Your Majesty's noble daughter, following in the footsteps of her sublime mother, does not have much time in order to avoid a disaster. How can this be ignored since I have had the pleasure and honor to see with my own eyes the most pure and ardent charity born, nurtured, and settled in her heart? But it is not enough that I pay attention to the unfortunate whose need for help is known. Something more is necessary. It is necessary that the entire nation know about this need and that Europe does not ignore it. When the Lord was leading his disciples he taught them that alms should be given to the poor in such a way that one hand does not know what the other hand has given. He spoke in this way to his disciples because they had no kings. A monarch is not a private person; he is a public person who not only does good in order to sanctify himself, but also so that others may be sanctified by his example.

The Spanish nation is lost as long as something does not violently put an end to the misguided inclinations of the comfortable classes, inclinations that can carry everyone into an abyss. Madam, this is not empty rhetoric: Spain is in a time like the last years of Louis Philippe[3] and on the eve of the cataclysm of February. I pray that something will happen here that has never before happened; that a great example will be given to the rich classes by the Throne. I pray that there will be no festivals. But if there are, may there be only a few of them and may they be exclusively for the poor. And instead of the great and costly festivals for the rich, there should be generous alms given, greater than those that have been given in other times and greater than what is thought appropriate on this occasion, in order to continue the custom of helping those in need. Perhaps this outstanding example of generosity and virtue will contribute to turning away the comfortable classes from the evil road they now follow so that they can return to the path of virtue and generosity. Madam, even if they all do not follow such an example, at least the Throne will be able to withstand the impetus of great hurricanes by following this course I recommend. The poor are God's friends. God will not permit the fall of a Throne upon which is seated a queen who is a mother and friend of the poor.

Christian monarchies have lasted for fourteen centuries because God has given them a sacred and mysterious virtue by dint of which they have been slowly and progressively adapting to the varied course of time. Even when all social ties were weak, the monarchy was strongly tied to the people. When insolent feudal barons were sacking cities, the people saw their kings as the symbols of justice. And because they knew how to satisfy all social necessities in different eras, in the beginning as strongmen and later as dispensers of justice, grateful peoples progressively acquired absolute kings.

Madam, today marks the beginning of a new era for princes. Unfortunate are those princes who do not know what is needed for these times. One cannot try to unite with a strong chain various nomadic tribes and warriors since nations are already definitively constituted. Nor can anyone leave the administration of justice in the hands of insolent barons who considered pillage and vengeance to be law. The administration of justice has left their hands forever and now rests in the hands of tribunes charged with correctly and impartially applying the law. The only thing that can be done today is to properly distribute wealth that is poorly distributed. Madam, this is the only matter agitating the world today. If the rulers of nations do not resolve this matter, socialism will come along and resolve it by looting the nations. Now, the problem has only one solution, only one peaceful solution, only one appropriate solution. The wealth accumulated through immense arrogance must be distributed through almsgiving on a grand scale.

I still have faith in the European monarchies, especially the Spanish monarchy. I cannot believe that on this occasion, for the first time in the long progression of the Catholic era, they will fail in the responsibility God has given them, the responsibility of being the most suitable institution that can better and more completely satisfy, due to its prodigious flexibility, all social necessities. The royal office becomes more difficult and painful every day. Now more than ever it can be said that reigning is a great act of self-denial and sublime sacrifice. It is not enough to be strong and just in order to reign. One must be charitable in order to be truly just and strong. Madam, charity is the virtue of saints. Today only saints can save nations that are afflicted with no other sickness, if one looks carefully, than the absence of Christian virtues. God does not permit the criminal impatience of the poor except as a punishment for the insolent egotism of the rich. Nor does he permit the criminal egotism of the rich except in order to castigate the needy who are carried away by their culpable impatience.

Since I am already writing a long letter, I will not lay down my pen until I have presented all of my thoughts to Your Majesty. I am not so destitute of reason that I propose to give myself more importance than I have. If the Spanish monarchy is sick (and it is, without any doubt, gravely sick), its cure can only come through the queen of Spain who gives royal alms instead of festivals. I am quite aware that (and how could I not be aware?) between the sickness and the remedy there is no due proportion. The monarchy will not save itself because it is splendid and generous with the poor on one occasion. The comfortable classes will not lose their egotism in one blow because their queen gave them the example of a grand munificence on one memorable day. The importance of this magnificent example is that it is the starting point of a new social era and of a new system of government. All of the great Catholic institutions have been falling, one after another, before the impetus of revolutions. May this example be the beginning of a complete restoration of all Catholic institutions in Spain.

The Catholic spirit has been dislodged by the revolutionary spirit of our political and economic legislation. May this example be the beginning of the complete restoration of the Catholic spirit in our economic and political legislation. The right of speaking to and teaching people, which the Church received from God himself through the apostles, has been usurped by a coterie of hidden journalists and most ignorant charlatans. This diminishes the grandeur of Spain. The ministry of the word, which is the most venerable as well as the most invincible of all ministries, has everywhere, since it has conquered the world, been changed from a ministry of salvation into an abominable ministry of ruin. Since nothing or no one could contain its triumphs in apostolic times, neither nothing nor no one, Madam, can today contain its ravages. The word has been, is now, and always will be the queen of the world. Society does not perish in any way except when the word of the Church, which is the word of life, is withdrawn. Societies are fallen and hungry because they do not receive their daily bread from the Church. Every proposal of salvation will be sterile if the great Catholic word is not fully restored. The last concordat is an excellent beginning for this restoration. But this is nothing more than an excellent beginning. I must not hide the truth from Your Majesty, the truth that is necessary in order to remove and change everything and tear down the revolutionary edifice, stone by stone.

Revolution has been definitely made by the rich and for the rich against kings and the poor. If I offer no proof of this it is not because it is difficult to prove, but because there would be so much needed in order to prove it. I will only content myself by observing that through the electoral census the poor have been socially marginalized. Strong in their impossible position, the rich have divided among themselves the spoils of convents. This was done by the rich claiming exclusive power for themselves, who then, as legislators, passed a law that doubled their wealth.. Since the day of the Creation until today, the world has not witnessed a more shameful example of audacity and greed. Madam, this helps to explain those great and sudden upheavals we all see with fearful eyes. What we see is not what we believe we are seeing. It is something else. We are seeing the wrath of God shaking the nations.

Among all errors, the most disastrous will be those that claim, as some now claim, that these fears are premature in Spain because there are no socialists in Spain. May it please Your Majesty not to believe in the importance of such extravagant claims. Just because there have been no socialists in Spain, that does not mean that what is happening here could not produce the same effects as socialism. Nor does it mean that socialism is not a contagious disease. Morever and above all else, what is happening here requires that Spain cease being a Catholic society. Socialism is a disease that indefectibly attacks, according to the design of God, every society that has been Catholic and has ceased being Catholic. And it attacks only societies that have been Catholic.

Madam, this is a new observation. But I hope that Your Majesty will permit me to say what is true and profound. God is mysteriously merciful to those who follow him, mildly just with those who ignore him, and merciless with those who know and yet despise him. For this reason he has placed his tabernacles of glory in Catholic nations, condemned pagan nations in the many events of their varied fortunes, and reserved socialism, the greatest of social disasters, for apostate nations. Spain will again be Catholic or will end up being socialist. Did I say it will be socialist? Madam, it is already socialist. Only it does not appear to be so because Spain does not know it. He who is consumptive suffers from consumption, even if he does not know what he is suffering because he is ignorant of the name of the disease.

The salvation of Spain and its glorious monarchy is at the end of the road I am quickly describing. Its salvation is only at the end of this road. Whether a ministry remains or vanishes; whether the Puritan or the conservative faction rules; whether a proper name is eclipsed or shines; whether in the pursuit of ministries fortune is declared for these or some other seekers, all of this is useless because the building is tumbling to the ground with a great uproar and scandal. God made nations curable. Only princes, not intrigues, have the divine power to cure sick nations.

Your Majesty is certainly able to understand the importance of these great principles. Your Majesty, you do not want to intervene in every matter of State. You cannot do this. Nor must you do this. Nevertheless, you can neither desire nor agree that the truth never be uttered in the high regions of politics and that the State miserably perish.

In great crises, and great is the crisis in which Europe now finds itself, there is no one who, in the given circumstances and with due circumspection, does not have the right and the duty of speaking the truth frankly and simply with a voice that is respectful as well as austere. Your Majesty has always been so good to me that I have never vacillated a single time in communicating to Your Majesty, even if briefly, what I think about affairs in Spain, of which Your Majesty, through love and goodness, is protector and mother. In writing this letter I do not arrive at a determined end. This letter is a conversation that, except for the distance, would have been spoken instead of written. Months ago I believed I could speak with the Duke.[4] Deprived of this last resource, I finally decided to write this letter, which I place under your benevolent protection.

May God give Your Majesty a long life and many happy years. Madam—at the royal feet of Your Majesty.

—Juan Donoso Cortés
Paris, 26 November 1851

NOTES

1. María Cristina (1806–1878) was the wife of King Fernando VII (1784–1833) and the mother of Queen Isabel II (1830–1904). Upon the death of Fernando in 1833 Isabel became queen of Spain at the age of three. Her mother, María Cristina, ruled as regent until 1843. Even after she stepped down as regent, María Cristina continued to be an influence on her daughter and thereby continued to be a powerful political player in Spain. This letter was an attempt to influence the young Queen Isabel through her mother.

2. Queen Isabel II.

3. Louis Philippe (1773–1850), the last king of France, was overthrown during the revolution of 1848.

4. The Infante Francisco de Asis, Duke of Cadiz, husband of Isabel II.

Letters to the Editor of *El Heraldo*

Paris, 15 April 1852

My dear Sir:

In the issue of your paper dated 8 April I read an article dedicated to the defense of *rationalism*, *liberalism*, and *parliamentarianism* as well as an elegy recounting all of the excellent qualities of discussion. To support your doctrines you quoted in this article certain words that I spoke in 1836 at the Ateneo in Madrid uttered against the divine right of kings. You called these words of mine eloquent and, even more, resounding.

I believe it is my duty to write you these short lines in order to remind you that the time has long passed for me to deserve such praise and to claim that you have either forgotten something or are censoring something. It must be said that there is a radical contradiction as well as an invincible repugnance between the doctrines you profess, and that I professed when I was much younger, and those that I now profess.

You believe that *rationalism* is the way to achieve what is reasonable; that *liberalism* in theory is the way to achieve *freedom* in practice; that *parliamentarianism* is the way to constitute a *good government*; that *discussion* is to truth what *means* are to *ends*; and finally, that kings are nothing more than the incarnation of *human rights*. Rights and the concentration of all rights are for God. *Duty* and the concentration of all duties are for man. Man calls his *right* the advantage that results from another's favorable compliance with duty. On his lips the word *right* is just a vicious expression. Later he transforms this vicious expression into a theory, a theory that unleashes storms upon the world.

I believe, as you well know, that discussion is the fount of all possible errors as well as the origin of all imaginable extravagances. I believe that *parliamentarianism*, *liberalism*, and *rationalism* are, first, a rejection of *government*; second, a rejection of *freedom*; and third, an affirmation of insanity.

So, what will I be asked if I am against discussion as it is understood by modern societies or if I am not a liberal, a rationalist, or a parliamentarian? Are you, perhaps, an absolutist?

I would be an absolutist if absolutism were the contradiction of all these things. But History teaches me that there are rationalist absolutisms and, up to a certain point, that there are liberal, argumentative, and parliamentary forms of absolutism. So, absolutism is, at best, contradictory in form. Yet it is not contradictory in the essence of those of its doctrines that have become famous due to the extent of their depravity. The doctrines of absolutism do not contradict its forms because it is impossible for there to be a contradiction between things of a different nature. What can be more absurd than finding that a *form* is radically contradictory to a *doctrine*, or that a *doctrine* is radically contradictory to a *form*?

Only Catholicism is the contradictory doctrine that combats these doctrines. You can think whatever you like about Catholic doctrine. In spite of what you think about it, everything will be instantly transformed and you will see the face of the earth renewed by it.

Within the Catholic doctrinal perspective every phenomenon is placed in an ordered hierarchy of phenomena and all things are placed in an ordered hierarchy of things. Reason parts company with *rationalism* (that is, a light which shines without being ignited by anyone) in order to be reason. It is a marvelous light that shines on itself and disseminates the splendid light of dogma, the most pure reflection of God, who is an eternal and uncreated light.

Freedom, as understood by Catholicism, is neither a right in its essence nor a contract in its form. It does not preserve itself by war. It is not a contract. And it is not acquired by conquest. It is not a priestess of Bacchus captivated by wine, like the freedom of demagogues. It does not noisily move among the nations like a queen, like parliamentary freedom. It does not have tribunes, who are its courtesans, as its servants. It is not made drowsy by the billing and cooing of the masses. It does not have permanent armies composed of national guards. And it is not pleased to softly recline itself in the triumphant coach of revolution.

Under the dominion of Catholicism God distributes his commandments, which are the bread of life to those who govern as well as to those who are governed, reserving to himself the inalienable right of being obeyed by the governed as well as by those who govern. This is a political matrimony celebrated between sovereign and subject in the presence and under the auspices of God. It is neither a sacrament nor a contract. Yet being holy, this matrimony resembles a sacrament more than a contract because it implicitly binds sovereign and subject together through the divine commandments.

According to these commandments the subject has the duty of lovingly obeying the sovereign that God establishes over him. The established sovereign governs his subjects that God has lovingly placed in his hands. When subjects fail to be lovingly obedient to their sovereigns, God permits the establishment of tyrannies. When a sovereign fails to be lovingly gentle, God permits revolutions. Tyrannies restore obedience among subjects. Revolutions restore sovereigns to gentleness. In this way God derives good out of the evil done by man. History, if it is examined well, is nothing more than the relationship of various events of the enormous struggle between good and evil, the divine will and human will, and a merciful God and rebellious man.

When God's commandments are exactly obeyed, when princes are lovingly gentle and subjects lovingly obedient, this simultaneous submission to all the divine commandments results in the existence of a certain social order, a certain manner of being, and a certain well-being that is individual as well as common. This is what I call the *state of freedom.* This is true freedom because justice reigns in this order. And it is justice that makes us free. This is freedom for the sons of God. This is Catholic freedom. This freedom is not defined, particular, or concrete. It is neither an organ of a political organism nor of various social institutions. It is not this; it is more than this. It is the general result of the good disposition of all organs and of the hegemony and harmony of all institutions. The health of the organism in general is more valuable than the health of a single organ. The overall life of a social and political body is more precious that the life of a flourishing institution.

Catholic freedom stands completely as one of the two most excellent things found anywhere. It is everywhere. This freedom is so holy and strong as well as fragile at the same time because every injustice offends it. It is shattered by everything that animates and produces the slightest movement of disorder. It is so loving that everyone is invited by its love. It is so gentle that everyone is offered its peace. It is so circumspect and modest that when Heaven came down to make many happy, it was acknowledged by only a few and applauded by no one. This freedom does not know what to call itself. Or, if it knows, it does not say so. And the world is ignorant of its name.

Concerning the matter of discussion, there is no greater similarity between Catholicism and philosophy than what is observed between Catholic freedom and what is called *political freedom.*

Catholicism proceeds in this way. It takes a ray of light that comes from above and gives it to man in order to make his reason fertile. This weak ray of light is converted into the luminous torrent that bathes the horizons by means of this fertilization. Philosophy, however, begins by artistically hiding the truth and light that have come from Heaven behind a dense veil. It poses an insoluble problem to reason in the following terms: through this fertilization truth and light are drawn from doubt and obscurity. This is the risk involved in the fertilization of human reason. In this way philosophy seeks a solution from man that he cannot give without a prior upheaval of eternal and immutable laws. According to these laws the fertilization of human reason is only powerful enough to develop the fertilized seed in conformity with the conditions of reason's own nature and consciousness. Thus the obscure proceeds from what is obscure, the luminous from what is luminous, the similar from what is similar. *Deum de Deo, lumen de lumine* (God from God, light from light.).

Obeying these laws, human reason fertilizes the doubt that comes from the rejection of reason. It also fertilizes the obscurity that comes from the palpable darkness. And it does this through the logical and progressive transformations found in the very nature of things.

Proceeding along such different paths, it is not at all strange that Catholicism and philosophy have been overrun by such different fortunes. For eighteen centuries Catholicism has been engaged in discussion in its own way. And the way it does this has made it victorious in every discussion.

Everything passes away before it: everything in time as well as time itself. Only Catholicism never passes away. It is exactly where God placed it, immovable in the midst of the enormous whirlwinds that stir up universal movement. Catholicism alone lives its own life without dying in this world of short lives. Death has not received permission to come near it, not even in those low and dark regions subject to its rule.

In order to review its forces, one day it said to itself: "I will choose a barbarian age and topple it with my miracles." Catholicism chose the eighteenth century and adorned it with the four most superb monuments to human genius: the *Summa theologiæ* of Saint Thomas; the laws of Castile of King Alfonso the Wise; the *Divine Comedy* of Dante; and the cathedral of Cologne.

For four thousand years rationalism has been discussing things in its own way. And it has also left behind two immortal monuments in order to immortalize its memory: the pantheon in which all philosophies repose and the pantheon in which all constitutions repose.

We do not need to speak about parliamentarianism. What can parliamentarianism be to a truly Catholic nation where man knows, from the day he is born, that he must give an account to God for every idle word?

I remain your attentive and true servant.

—Juan Donoso Cortés

Paris, 30 April 1852

My dear Sir:

I am sending these lines to you for two reasons: first, in order to thank you for having given generous and courteous hospitality to my previous letter and for having responded reasonably to it, which is something rather rare in these rationalist times; second, in order to correct some equivocations that have appeared in *El Heraldo* as well as in those papers that have had the pleasure of disputing with me.

It is first supposed that I am an enemy of all discussion. I am only the enemy of a *certain manner* of discussion. The proof of this is that I am a great devotee of the fathers and doctors of the Church who spent their lives in discussions. And I am a devotee of the Church which has always been dogmatic as well as engaged in discussion at the same time.

Second, it is greatly supposed that I am fond of engaging in the same discussions that I condemn in theory. The contrary is true. I do not deny that I am fond of plainly expounding upon my doctrines. But, in general, I neither seek nor approve of discussion since I am convinced that it quickly degenerates into disputes, which always harm charity by inflaming passions and thereby causing the contenders to fail in three great respects: in what a man owes to other men, to the truth, and to himself. Words are like seeds. I throw them into the wind and leave them to God's care, to him who is Lord of the winds that rise up so that they can fall according to his will on sterile rocks or on fertile ground.

Third, it is said that I am opposed to *parliaments* because I oppose *parliamentarianism.* Parliamentarianism is a false *doctrine* that has nothing to do with parliaments, which are indifferent *forms.* If I was an enemy of parliaments, as I am of parliamentarianism, I would not be able to entrust this declaration to my benevolent commentators. Everyone knows that I am undaunted in declaring my principles and that I value my own opinions.

Fourth, it is said that I justify revolutions and tyrannies in a certain way. I have not done this except in order to explain these unjustifiable phenomena. I have stated that God permits them, just as he permits the evil that he condemns. I have never said that I approve of them like I approve of the *good* that God does. God greatly approves of the good that results from and that can be obtained from these evils. What is good is the correction that disobedient peoples receive from tyrants and that tyrants receive from revolutions. What is good in this evil is not the evil itself, which is always bad, but the effect that is a great warning to demagogues and tyrants. If there is one person in the world who rises in revolt against and who, besides himself, mentions these two monsters of the human race, it is me. And still I am misunderstood, even by those who support me.

My theory on freedom seems utopian to you, and it is. The equivocation here is not in your judgment about it. It is in supposing that all theories are not utopian, including parliamentarian, socialist, and constitutional theories. Never in the world, or in any era of History, has a theory exactly corresponded to practice in government. A theory only contains the utopian ideal of what is practiced. Now, from theory to theory, utopia to utopia, I prefer the theories and utopias of Ledru-Rollin[1] to those of Benjamin Constant[2] and those of Our Lord Jesus Christ to those of Proudhon. But, until the end I shall ask: When that beautiful Catholic freedom does not exist, what happens? This is what happens! Freedom is found in and relegated to the turbulent ebb and flow of tyrannies and revolutions. I cannot see how anything else can happen. I know that there are others who are more inventive. What I greatly doubt is the worth of their inventions. And is it not believed, as some papers have in good faith believed, that I propose revolutions and tyrannies as remedies? The only thing I have done is to record the historical facts that these phenomena always produce that cause peoples to depart from Catholic ways. I have done this in order to discover what they must do so that they can return to those ways and thereby avoid disasters.

Any attempt to avoid disasters by taking another route appears vain to me beyond any shadow of doubt. This is so because there is an inviolable law of the moral world stating that when societies do not obey the law of God, they are handed over to the brutality of facts. It is worth observing that all peoples who wanted to invent rather than receive the truth, that is, all who departed from being *truly* Catholic in order to be *purely partisans of discussion*, have ended up falling under the yoke of horrible dictatorships and brutal facts. England is no exception to this. This general rule may imperfectly apply to it only because the torrent of discussion has always been contained by the powerful dikes of historical traditions. However, no truly Catholic people has ever known for a long time either the dictatorship of brutal facts or the brutal fact of dictatorship.

Two things have been charged against me: first, that I advise preaching about duty and not its fulfillment; second, that I claim that all human institutions are useless. Concerning the first charge, it is enough to convince oneself that it is baseless by again reading my letter. Concerning the second charge, it will suffice to observe here that I do not believe that those institutions directed towards the fulfillment of duties are useless. I applaud all those institutions that fulfill such a function, social ones as well as the most august and holy ones. Furthermore, I say that of the various institutions that have been known in History, I do not condemn any of them if they receive their soul and life from Catholic truth.

If after these simple explanations there are still those who believe that I condemn what I have not condemned and applaud what I have not applauded, I abandon such unhappy ones to God and to their consciences.

Since it is not my intention to enter into any sort of discussion, except in order to briefly rectify some facts, I shall end my letter. However, I will not do this without expressing my gratitude to all those papers (even to the most outrageous ones) that have occupied themselves with the letter I previously sent to you. It must not be believed that those papers have no merit if I forget them. All that is wrong here is a loss of memory. What can be done if I forget them?

I remain your attentive servant.

—Juan Donoso Cortés

NOTES

1. Alexandre Auguste Ledru-Rollin (1807–1874), influential French political figure who was a militant advocate of republicanism. He was a leader in the revolution of February 1848 that overthrew King Louis Philippe and the restored French monarchy and established the Second Republic. See Alvin R.Calman, *Ledru-Rollin and the Second French Republic* (New York: Octagon Books, 1980).

2. Benjamin Constant (1767–1830), French-Swiss political writer and novelist. He became interested in politics through the influence of Germaine de Staël. His affair with her took him to Paris (1795). He served as a tribune under Napoleon I (1799–1801) but lived in exile with de Staël (1802–1814) after she was expelled from France. During the restoration of the Bourbon dynasty he served in the chamber of deputies (1819–1822, 1824–1830), earning a reputation as a liberal.

Letter to Cardinal Fornari on the Errors of Our Times

Your Eminence,

Before submitting these brief remarks to you in compliance with the request you addressed to me in your letter of last May, it seems appropriate for me to indicate the limits I have placed upon myself in their composition.[1]

Among the contemporary errors, there is not a single one which is not already found among the heresies that have already been condemned by the Church. The Church has condemned all present and future errors in the errors of the past that have already been condemned. The errors of the present and the past are identical when we examine their nature and origin. But when we view them in their applications, they present us with a spectacle of ominous variety. Today I propose to consider them from the perspective of their applications rather than from their nature and origin. This means I am considering them from the political and social perspective, not the purely religious perspective; from the perspective of their variety, not from what they have that makes them identical; from what they have that is mutable, not immutable. Two important considerations have influenced me to take this route. One concerns my own personal circumstances. The other concerns the actual nature of the age in which we live. Concerning myself, I have held that my position as a public figure and a layman obliges me to reject my own competence in resolving those fearful questions pertaining to the articles of our faith and dogmatic matters. Concerning the age in which we live, there is nothing better than to examine it in order to know that what makes it sadly famous among all ages is precisely not the arrogance with which it proclaims its heresies and errors, but, rather, the satanic audacity in how it applies these heresies and errors, that have been defeated in past ages, in our society today.

There was a time when human reason, delighting itself with insane speculations, was satisfied when it successfully opposed a denial to an affirmation in the intellectual sphere; when it successfully opposed an error to a truth among metaphysical ideas; and when it successfully opposed a heresy to a dogma in the religious sphere. Today this same reason does not remain satisfied if it does not descend into the political and social spheres in order to disturb everything. It is enchanted with causing conflict by spreading error, fomenting revolution through the spread of heresy, and precipitating an enormous disaster through the spread of its arrogant denials.

Today the tree of error appears to have reached its providential maturity. It was planted by the first generation of heretics. Then it was watered by other heretics in succeeding generations. It dressed itself with leaves in the time of our grandfathers. And it was covered with flowers in the days of our fathers. Today it is before us full of fruit within the reach of our hands. Its fruit is very bad, as was its flowers, which perfumed it in former times, the leaves that dressed it, the trunk that sustained it, and the men who planted it. I do not want to say that what has already been condemned at one time must not be condemned again. I only want to say that a *special* condemnation, analogous to the *special* transformation of these ancient errors before our eyes today, appears absolutely necessary. It is from this perspective that I see myself as having any competence in the matter at hand.

Thus discarding with purely theological considerations, I have focused my attention on those matters which, being theological in their origin and essence, have gradually become, nevertheless, political and social in scope. Yet even among these considerations, I have found it necessary to disregard certain ones that appear to me to be of lesser importance due to a lack of time as well as to the excessive demands of my own occupations. However, I believe it is my duty to touch on some matters upon which I have not been consulted.

Also, due to a lack of time and the excessive demands of my occupations, it has been impossible for me to reread the works of the modern heretics in order to identify the propositions that must be fought and condemned in them. However, by attentively considering this particular point, I am convinced that in times past this was more necessary than it is today, even though, if one pays close attention, these times have one notable difference about them. In the past, if errors of any kind could not be found anywhere except in books, they could not be found. In our own times, however, error is found in books and everywhere else because it is everywhere. Error can be found in books, institutions, journals, speeches, conversations, classrooms, homes, forums, in whatever is said as well as in whatever is not said. Pressed by time, I have inquired about what is nearest to me, and the atmosphere has responded.

The errors circulating today are infinite in number. But if you look closely, all of them originate and end in two supreme denials, one relative to God and the other to man. Society denies that God cares for his creatures and that man is conceived in sin. In its pride it has said two things to the man of these times, and both have been believed: man is flawless and does not need God; man is strong and handsome, so we see him arrogant in his power and enamored with his beauty.

If we grant the denial of sin, the following, among many other things, are denied. We deny that temporal life is one of expiation and that the world in which this life is passed is a valley of tears; that the light of reason is frail and vacillating; that the will of man is infirm; that pleasure has been given to us as a temptation in order to free us from its attractiveness; that pain is a good when it is voluntarily accepted for a supernatural motive; that time has been given to us for our salvation; and that man needs to be sanctified.

If we grant these denials, among many other things come the following consequences: temporal life is given to us in order to elevate ourselves to the highest perfection by our own efforts and by means of an undefined progress; the place in which this life is passed can and must be transformed by man; there is no truth that cannot be grasped due to the sane reason of man; and it is not true that man's reason does not grasp anything. It also follows that there is no other evil except that which man's reason tells him is such. Thus there is no other evil or sin except philosophical evil and sin. The will of man is correct in itself and, therefore, does not need correction. Man must avoid pain and seek pleasure. Time has been given to man in order for him to enjoy it. And man is good and sane in himself.

These denials and affirmations lead to further analagous ones with respect to God. In supposing that man has not fallen, one proceeds to deny, and does deny, the notion that man has been restored as well as the mystery of the Redemption and Incarnation—the dogma of the external personality of the Word and the Word itself. If we grant, on one side, the natural integrity of the human will, and, on the other side, nonexistence of any other evil and sin except philosophical evil and sin, one proceeds to deny, and does deny, the sanctifying action of God over man. And with that, one also denies the dogma of the personality of the Holy Spirit. All these denials culminate in the denial of the sovereign dogma of the Holy Trinity, the cornerstone of our faith and the foundation of all Catholic dogmas.

Out of this a vast system of naturalism originates and is born, a system that is a radical, universal, and absolute contradiction of all our beliefs. We Catholics believe and profess that sinful man is in perpetual need of aid and that God perpetually grants this aid through his supernatural assistance, a marvelous work of his infinite love and mercy. The supernatural is the atmosphere of the natural for us; that is, the supernatural simultaneously envelopes and sustains the natural without being noticed.

There was once a fathomless abyss between God and man. But the son of God was made man. And since the divine nature and human nature are united in him, the abyss was filled. However, there was still an immense distance between the Divine Word, that is God as well as man, and sinful man. God placed the mother of his son—the most Holy Virgin, the woman without sin—between his Son and his creature in order to shorten this immense distance. The distance between the woman without sin and sinful man was still great. So God, in his infinite mercy, placed the saints between the Blessed Virgin and sinful man.

Who cannot admire such a great, wonderful, sovereign, and perfect scheme? The greatest sinner need not do anything more than extend his sinful hand in order to encounter the one who helps him to climb, step by step, to the heights of Heaven from the abyss of his sins.

To a certain extent, these are nothing more than visible and external forms, visible and external to the extraordinary effects of that supernatural aid given by God to rescue man so that he may tread the rugged path of life with a firm footing. It is necessary to probe the highest and most hidden regions with the eyes of faith in order to form an idea about this wonderful supernaturalism and see the Church as being perpetually moved by the most secret action of the Holy Spirit. It is necessary to probe that most secret of sanctuaries, the soul, and see how the grace of God implores and seeks it; how the soul of a man opens and closes its ear to that divine call; and how that grace commences and continually pursues a silent dialogue between the creature and his Creator. On the other hand, it is necessary to see what the spirit of darkness does, says, and seeks in the soul. And it is necessary to see how the soul of a man comes and goes, is agitated, and toils between two eternities in order to finally fall into the regions of light or darkness according to the spirit it follows.

We need to look and see how the guardian angel at our side exposes deplorable thoughts so that they cannot molest us as well as how he places his hands under our feet so that we will not stumble. It is necessary that we examine History and see the wonderful manner in which God disposes of human events for his glory and for the good of his elect. Because God is master of these events, man must cease trying to be the master of his own actions. We must see how God sustains conquerors, conquests, captains, and wars at opportune times; how he restores and pacifies everything at the same time, demolishing warriors and subduing the pride of conquerors; how he permits tyrants to rise against sinful people and how he sometimes consents to rebellious peoples being the lash used upon tyrants; how he reunites tribes, separates castes, or disperses nations; how he gives and takes away the empires of the earth according to his own fancy; how he knocks them to the ground and elevates them to the heavens. Finally, we must see how men confusedly and blindly traverse the labyrinth of History that each generation of human beings keeps building without being able to identify its structure, its entrance, or its exit.

This entire, vast, and splendid supernatural system, which is the universal key and explanation of all things human, is implicitly or explicitly rejected by those who affirm the immaculate conception of man. And those who today affirm this are not only a few philosophers, but also the rulers of nations, the influential classes of society, and even society itself, poisoned with the venom of this irksome heresy.

We find here the explanation of everything we see and touch. At this point we must pause to consider the following arguments. If the light of our reason has not been darkened, it is sufficient, without the help of faith, in order to discover the truth. If faith is not necessary, reason is sovereign and independent. The progress of the truth depends upon the progress of reason. The progress of reason depends upon its exercise. And its exercise depends upon discussion. Therefore, discussion is the true and fundamental law of modern societies as well as the only crucible where truths are separated from errors after they are melted down. From this principle comes such notions as the freedom of the press, the inviolability of the tribunal, and the royal sovereignty of deliberative assemblies.

If the will of man is not infirm, the attractiveness of the good is alone sufficient in order for it to follow the good without the help of supernatural grace. If man does not need this assistance, he also does not need the sacraments that have been given to him or the prayers procured for him. If prayer is not necessary, then it is wasteful. And if it is wasteful, then the contemplative life and most religious communities are wasteful and useless. This demonstrates that wherever these ideas have penetrated, religious communities have been extinguished. If man does not need the sacraments, he also does not need those who administer them. And if he has no need for God, he also has no need for mediators. Where these ideas have taken root there emerges a contempt for and the proscription of the priesthood. Contempt for the priesthood always results in a contempt for the Church. And contempt for the Church is always the same as contempt for God.

If the action of God over man is denied, and if the fathomless abyss is again opened between the Creator and his creature (as far as this is possible), then, the Church is separated from society by the same distance at the same time. So, with God relegated to Heaven, the Church is relegated to the sanctuary. However, where man lives subject to the dominion of God, he is also naturally and instinctively subject to the dominion of his Church. The centuries testify to this truth. And this is confirmed in the present century as it was in the past.

Thus discarding all that is supernatural and converting religion into a vague sort of deism, the man who has no need for the Church, hidden away in its sanctuary, or of God, fixed in his Heaven like Jealousy to her rock, moves his eyes to the earth and consecrates himself exclusively to material interests.

This is the era of utilitarian systems, great commercial expansion, industrial fever, the insolence of the rich, and the impatience of the poor. This state of material wealth and religious indigence is always followed by one of those enormous disasters that tradition and History constantly engrave upon the human memory. The prudent and wise meet in council in order to ward off this disaster. The hurricane, which comes bellowing, suddenly disperses the council along with its supplications.

This makes it totally impossible to impede the invasion of revolutions and the advent of tyranny. These events are identical because they both result in the domination of force when they have relegated the Church to the sanctuary and God to Heaven. The intent of the public powers to artificially fill the great void left in society by the absence of God and the Church is vain and ridiculously presumptuous. In the absence of those vital spirits, the force of industry wants to reproduce the phenomena of life by purely mechanical means. Since neither the Church nor God are forms, there is no form that can occupy that great void when they are withdrawn from society. On the contrary, no government is essentially dangerous when God and his Church operate freely if, on the part of society, customs are friendly and the times favorable.

There is no accusation more remarkable and strange than the one circulated by certain schools of opinion and thought claiming that Catholicism, on the one hand, favors government by the masses. On the other hand, there are other sectarians who claim that Catholicism is an impediment to the advancement of freedom since it favors the expansion of vast tyrannies. How can anything be more absurd than the first accusation, especially since Catholicism has constantly condemned rebellion while sanctifying obedience as the common obligation of all men? What can be more absurd than the second accusation, especially since the Catholic religion is the only one which teaches that no man has rights over another, because all authority comes from God; because nothing that is small in God's eyes can be great; because all power is instituted for the good; because commanding is the same as serving; and because the rule of a prince is a mystery and, consequently, a sacrifice?

These fundamental principles, revealed by God's Holy Church, constitute the public law of all Christian nations. This public law is the incessant affirmation of true freedom, because it is a constant negation and condemnation of the right of princes to convert their power into tyranny. Freedom consists precisely in the denial of this right. Freedom consists in this denial. Freedom is impossible without it. If we look at this more closely, the affirmation of freedom and the denial of this right are two different ways of saying the same thing. Thus, it follows that Catholicism not only is not a friend of revolutions and tyrannies, but that it has also found in this same negation the proper nature of true freedom.

Nor is it less absurd to suppose, as some do, that the holy religion we profess, and the Church it resides in and that preaches it, checks or looks with coolness upon the unfettered expansion of public wealth, sound solutions to economic problems, and the increase of material interests because it does not propose to make people powerful, only blessed; or because the Church does not make men wealthy, but only holy. This is simply one of its great and noble teachings revealing the divine charge given to man to transform Nature so that it serves him through his work.

The Church seeks a certain equilibrium between material interests and moral and religious interests. In this equilibrium it seeks that primacy of place be given to moral and religious interests. Material interests are secondary. This is the correct order of things because reason tells us and History teaches us that this order, which is the necessary condition for this equilibrium, is the only one that can ward off, and certainly does ward off, great disasters, which are always ready to arise whenever the exclusive influence and increase of material interests incite concupiscence.

Others are persuaded, on the one hand, that in order not to perish they have need in this life for the aid of our holy religion and Church. On the other hand, though, they sadly submit themselves to its yoke, which is light for those who are humble and heavy for those who are swollen with pride. They seek to separate themselves from our religion and Church by accepting some of the Church's teachings while rejecting teachings they consider to be too extreme. This stance is much more dangerous when it assumes the guise of a proper impartiality in order to win over and seduce nations. In this way truth and error are obliged to stand before a judge in order to seek an impossible mean between them through a false moderation. It is certain that truth is in the habit of being encountered, and is encountered, among errors. However, there is no mean between truth and error. There is only an immense void between these two contrary poles. What is in the void is just as far from truth as it is from error. In the truth there is nothing except that which is embraced with it.

These are the principle errors of the men and classes to whom has fallen the sad privilege of governing nations in our times. Turning our attention to the other side, to those who are taking the lead in reclaiming the inheritance of governing, we see that their reason is disturbed and their imagination confounded as they encounter ever more pernicious and abominable errors. Nevertheless, it is worth observing, that these most pernicious and abominable errors are nothing more that the logical consequences of the above mentioned errors.

Supposing the immaculate conception of man, and with it the integral beauty of nature, some ask: "If our reason is luminous and our will correct and excellent, why have our passions, which are in our will and reason, not become most excellent?" Others ask: "If discussion is good for arriving at truth, then why are some things not under truth's sovereign jurisdiction?" Still others are unable to grasp anything with their reason because the freedoms to think, desire, and work are not absolute, as was previously supposed.

In religious controversies questions are posed in an effort to ascertain why God is allowed into Heaven if he is useless in society, and why the sanctuary is permitted if the Church is of no use to society. Others ask, since progress toward the good is not definite, why is one not supposed to attack the feat of raising enjoyments to the level of concupiscence and of changing this tearful valley into a garden of delights? Philanthropists show themselves to be scandalized when they encounter the poor on the streets. They are not able to grasp how a pauper who is so ugly can be a man, or how a man who is so handsome can be so poor. However, they are able to clearly grasp, without any disagreements among themselves, the imperious need to subvert society, suppress governments, transfer riches, and eliminate all human and divine institutions with a single blow.

Even though it appears impossible, there is still an error that, considered in itself, is not detestable. Nevertheless, it is of greater consequence than the above mentioned errors. This is the error of those who believe that these errors do not necessarily and inevitably give birth to other errors. Humanly speaking, a society is lost if it does not quickly abandon this deviation from truth with a radical and sovereign condemnation. And it is also lost if in abandoning this deviation it does not condemn its consequent errors.

He who reads that most imperfect catalogue which lists these atrocious errors will observe that some result in an absolute state of confusion and anarchy, while others necessitate the realization of a despotism of unheard of and immense proportions. Those errors that sow confusion and anarchy pertain to the exaltation of human freedom as well as to the most violent destruction of all institutions. And those errors that result in despotism correspond to those that suppose an organized ambition.

According to the dialectical school of thought, those who are called socialists are the sectarians of the former. Communists are the sectarians of the latter. Socialists, above all, seek the undetermined expansion of individual human freedom at the expense of suppressed public authority. Communists, on the other hand, direct themselves to the complete suppression of human freedom and to the immense expansion of the authority of the State. The most complete formula of socialist doctrines is found in the writings of Girardin[2] and Proudhon. Girardin has discovered the centrifugal force and Proudhon the centripetal force of the future society that is to be governed by socialist ideas and will be obedient to two contrary movements: one of repulsion, produced by absolute liberty, and one of attraction, produced by a whirlwind of contracts. The essence of communism consists in the confiscation of all freedoms and of all other things that are good for the State.

What is so stupendous and monstrous about all these errors is that they come from the most astonishing of religious errors. They originate from and are explained by this error. The socialists are not content with relegating God to Heaven. They go beyond that by making a public profession of atheism and by completely denying him. Given the denial of God, who is the fount and origin of all authority, logic demands the absolute denial of authority itself. The denial of universal paternity leads to the denial of domestic paternity. And the denial of religious authority leads to the denial of political authority. When man is without God he is at the point of being a subject without a king and a son without a father.

It appears evident to me that communism proceeds from pantheism and other related heresies. When God is everything and everything is God, God is, above all, democracy and the masses. Individual persons, who are only divine atoms, emanate from a whole that perpetually engenders them so that they can return to the same whole, which also perpetually absorbs them. In this system, that which is not of the whole is not God, even though it participates in the divinity. That which is not God is nothing, because there is nothing outside of God, who is the whole. Thus arises a haughty contempt for man and an insolent denial of human freedom by the communists. Thus arises those immense aspirations to universal domination through a demagogy that must extend itself to all continents and touch the ultimate limits of the earth. And thus arises that senseless fury through which the communists propose to confound and crush all families, classes, nations, and races of people in their great mortar.

A God must some day emerge from this most dark and bloody chaos as the victor over all that is varied. This will be a universal God who will be the victor over all that is particular. And this will be an eternal God, without beginning or end, who will be the victor over all that is born and passes away. This God is demagogy, the God announced by the last prophets, the unique son of the future firmament, the one who must come carried by a tempest, crowned with rays of light, and served by hurricanes. This is the true whole, the true God, armed with only one attribute—omnipotence. And this God will be victorious over the three weaknesses of the Catholic God: good will, love, and mercy. Who will not recognize Lucifer in this God, the God of pride?

When these abominable doctrines are carefully examined, it is impossible not to see the mysterious, but visible, sign which these errors must convey in apocalyptic times. If a religious fear does not impede me from seeing these formidable times, it will not be difficult for me to support the opinion, with analogous reasons, that the great anti-Christian empire will be an enormous demagogic empire, ruled by a great satanic plebeian who will be the man of sin.

After having generally examined the principle errors of these times, and after having completely demonstrated that they originate in some religious error, it appears appropriate, as well as necessary, to investigate some applications that clearly demonstrate how all political and social errors are derived from religious errors. For example, all that affects the government of God over man undoubtedly affects the governments instituted in civil society in the same degree and manner.

The first religious error to emerge in recent times is the principle of the independence and sovereignty of human reason. To this religious error corresponds the political error that affirms the sovereignty of the human intellect. The sovereignty of the human intellect has been the universal foundation of public law since the first revolutions. Parliamentary monarchies, with their electoral census, division of powers, free press, and inviolable tribunals, originate in this error.

The second religious error is related to the human will and consists in affirming that the will is sound in itself and needs neither the call nor the stimulus of grace in order to incline it toward the good. The corresponding political error asserts that since there is no such thing as a sound will, nothing needs to be directed since there is no need for a director. Universal suffrage is founded on this principle and the republican system proceeds from it.

The third religious error pertains to the appetites and claims that the appetites of man are excellent. This presumes the immaculate conception of man. The corresponding political error asserts that all governments have one sole end: the satisfaction of all forms of concupiscence. The socialist and demagogic systems are founded upon this principle. And these are the very systems that today are struggling to dominate the world and which will eventually prevail while following the banners they raise in the natural course of events.

We cannot know what is religiously affirmed about God without also knowing what is politically affirmed or denied about government. When a vague deism prevails in religion, it is affirmed that God reigns over all creation while it is denied that he governs it. The political implications of this error are expressed in the parliamentary maxim asserting that *the king reigns but does not govern.*

When the existence of God is denied, everything concerning government is also denied, even existence itself. In these evil times the anarchical schools of socialism rise up and propagate themselves with frightful rapidity.

Finally, when the ideas of divinity and creation are confused to the point of asserting that created things are God, and God is the universe of created things, communism prevails in the political order; and pantheism prevails in the religious order. And God, tired of suffering, delivers man up to the mercy of contemptible and abominable tyrants.

Let us return now to the Church. It will be simple for me to demonstrate that it has been the object of the same errors. These errors always preserve their indestructible identity regardless of whether they are applied to God, to disturbing his Church, or upsetting civil societies.

The Church can be considered in two different ways: in itself as an independent and perfect society which has all it needs in order to work with ease and amply move itself and in its relations with civil societies and temporal governments.

Seen from the perspective of its internal organization, the Church has deemed it necessary to resist the great flood of pernicious errors. It has taken notice of the most harmful among them, those that are directed against what is marvelous and perfect about its unity, that is, the Pontificate, that fundamental rock of this prodigious edifice. Among these errors is that which denies the unique and indivisible succession of apostolic power over universal matters to the Vicar of Christ on earth, assuming that all the bishops are co-inheritors of this power. This error, if it could prevail, would introduce confusion and disunity in the Church of Our Lord, converting it through this multiplication of the Pontificate—which is the essential, indivisible, and incommunicable authority—into a turbulent aristocracy. Keeping the honor of a vain presidency, while real jurisdiction and effective government are gone from it, the Supreme Pontiff, under the rule of this deistic error, would be uselessly consigned to the Vatican, like God is uselessly consigned to Heaven, and like a king who is uselessly consigned to his throne under the rule of the error of parliamentarianism.

Those who live on bad terms with the rule of reason, which is aristocratic, prefer the rule of the will, which is democratic. They embrace presbyterianism, which is the Republic in the Church, just as they embrace universal suffrage, which is the Republic in civil society. Those who are smitten with the freedom of the individual exaggerate it to the point of proclaiming its all-embracing sovereignty as well as the destruction of all penal institutions. In civil matters they embrace the contractual society of Proudhon. They embrace individual inspiration in religious matters, something that was proclaimed as a dogma by some fanatical sectarians in the religious wars of England and Germany. Finally, those seduced by the errors of pantheism at last embrace the undivided sovereignty of the masses of the faithful in the ecclesiastical order, just as they embrace the divinization of all things in the divine order and the universal and absorbent sovereignty of compact groups in the civil order.

All of these errors pertaining to the hierarchical order established by God himself in his Church, most important because they are in the domain of speculation, greatly lose their importance in the domain of facts because it is absolutely impossible that they prevail in a society protected from their ravages by divine promises. The same thing can be said about those errors concerning the relations between the Church and civil society as well as between the priesthood and the Empire. Those errors were powerful in other centuries disturbing the peace of nations. And they are still with us today. However, since they are trying to impede the irresistible expansion of the Church over the world, they merely place obstacles before it and try to delay the day when the Church's confines are the very limits of the world itself.

There are several types of errors, depending upon what is asserted about the Church: whether it is equal to the State, inferior to the State, or serves no purpose at all. The first type of error is properly asserted by the most lukewarm of royalists. The second type pertains to the most ardent royalists. And the third type pertain to revolutionaries, who propose the ultimate outcome of royalism as the first premise of their arguments. The last type pertains to the socialists and the communists (that is, all the radical schools) and takes the ultimate outcome of the revolutionaries as the first premise for its argument.

The theory of equality between the Church and the State gives occasion to the most lukewarm of royalists to proclaim what there is in the nature of the laity that is of a mixed nature, and what there is in that mixed nature pertaining to the ecclesiastical nature. These assumptions are required in order to produce the endowment or patrimony that the State contributes to this egalitarian society. In such a society almost everything is disputable; and all that is disputable is resolved through agreements or concordats. In this system there emerges the common right, in the name of the State, to promulgate, as well as oversee, inspect, and censure bulls and apostolic letters issued by the Church.

The theory stating that no church can be identified with the State allows revolutionaries to proclaim the absolute separation between Church and State. The principle of the maintenance of the clergy and the conservation of cult exclusively by the faithful is a necessary consequence of this separation. The error asserting that the Church serves no purpose, which is a denial of the Church itself, gives rise to the violent suppression of the priesthood by a decree that naturally sanctions religious persecution.

It is certain that these errors are just reproductions of errors we have already identified in other areas. Just as the coexistence of Church and State results in these erroneous assertions and denials, so in the political order the same thing must occur regarding the coexistence of individual freedom and public authority. This happens again in the moral order concerning the coexistence of reason and faith; and in the historical order concerning the coexistence of Divine Providence and human freedom. In the highest regions of speculation, the destruction of the coexistence of the natural and supernatural order—the coexistence of two worlds—also occurs.

All these errors, identical in nature but varied in their applications, fatefully produce the same results in all their applications. When they are applied to the coexistence of individual freedom and public authority they produce war, anarchy, and revolutions in the State. When free will and grace become their objects, they first produce division and war within the person, then the anarchical exaltation of free will, and later the tyranny of concupiscence in the hearts of men.

When they are applied to reason and faith they first produce war between these two realms, then disorder, anarchy, and giddiness in the regions of the human intellect. When applied to the human intellect and God's Providence, they produce all the disasters throughout History. Finally, when they are applied to the coexistence of the natural and supernatural orders, anarchy, confusion, and war are prolonged in all spheres and regions.

Certainly, in the last analysis and final result, all these errors, in their quasi-infinite variety, resolve themselves into one error. This error consists in obscuring and falsifying the hierarchical order, which is immutable in itself, that God has placed in all things. This order resides in the hierarchical superiority of all that is supernatural over all things natural and, consequently, in the hierarchical superiority of faith over reason, grace over free will, divine Providence over human freedom, and the Church over the State. Simply stated, this hierarchical superiority concludes in the superiority of God over man.

The right claimed by faith to illuminate reason and guide it is not a usurpation. It is a prerogative conforming to the excellent nature of faith. On the contrary, the prerogative claimed by reason to set the limits of and domain of faith is not a right, but an ambitious pretension which does not conform to its inferior and subordinate nature. Submission to the secret inspirations of grace conforms to the universal order because it is merely a submission to divine claims and calls. And, furthermore, scorn, denial, or rebellion against grace places free will in an internal state of indigence and an external state of rebellion against the Holy Spirit.

The absolute lordship of God over all the great historical events he produces and permits is his incommunicable prerogative because History is like the mirror in which God externally views his designs. The pretension of man, when he asserts that he produces these events and weaves the marvelous cloth of History, is an unsustainable pretension because he can do nothing by himself but weave the cloth of his own actions, which are contrary to the divine commandments. Man needs help when weaving that cloth of those other actions of his which conform to the divine will.

The superiority of the Church over civil societies conforms to right reason which teaches us that that supernatural is *over the natural* and the divine is over the human. On the other hand, every aspiration on the part of the State to absorb the Church, or to make itself the Church's equal, is an anarchical aspiration impregnated with disasters and is a cause of conflicts.

The salvation of human societies exclusively depends upon the restoration of these political and social principles. However, these principles cannot be restored by anyone except those who know them. And no one can know then except those who are in the Catholic Church. The right of the Church to teach all nations, which comes from its founder and master, is not solely based upon this divine origin, but is also justified by that principle of right reason through which it imparts learning to the ignorant and teaches the most wise.

Even if the Church had not received this sovereign ministry from the Lord, it would still be authorized to exercise it based on the sole fact that it is the repository of the only principles that have that secret and marvelous virtue of maintaining all things in order and concert. And because it is the repository of such principles, it has the right of putting all things in order and concert. It is legitimate and reasonable to assert that the Church has the right to teach. But that assertion is incomplete if we do not assert that the world has the right to be taught by the Church.

Without a doubt, civil societies possess that tremendous power not to climb the highest mountains of eternal truths and of softly slipping, and even falling, into the abyss of the sloping rapids of error. But it must be determined if, when reason is lost, societies commit stupid acts when they exercise a right. Or, to put it another way, it must be determined whether or not societies exercise any rights when they renounce all rights by committing suicide.

The question of teaching, in recent times a matter of contention between academicians and French Catholics, has not been framed by the latter in its true terms. The universal Church cannot accept the terms that have been framed. On one side the freedom of cults is assumed. On the other side, the special circumstances of the French nation is assumed. It can be clearly seen that French Catholics have not been able to claim anything for the Church except freedom, which is a common right that can serve the Church as a protection and refuge for Catholic truth. However, the principle of the freedom of teaching, considered in itself, and abstracted from the special circumstances here stated, is a false principle and cannot possibly be accepted by the Catholic Church.

The Church cannot accept this freedom of teaching without contradicting all of its doctrines. In effect, proclaiming that teaching must be free leads to nothing other than the proclamation that there is no truth already known and which must be taught; that truth has not been encountered; that truth can only be found through an ample discussion of all opinions.

By proclaiming that teaching must be free, one is saying that truth and error have equal rights. So, on the one hand, the Church professes the principle that truth exists without any need to seek it. On the other hand, it professes that error is born without rights, lives without rights, dies without rights, and, therefore, the truth possesses absolute rights. The Church, then, by not accepting freedom, especially where it is not possible, cannot accept it as the end of its desires nor salute it as a unique mark of its aspirations.

These are the comments which I believe I am bound by duty to make concerning the most pernicious of the contemporary errors. To my own understanding, two things must be admitted if we impartially examine these errors: first, all errors have the same origin and center; second, all errors are religious when considered in terms of their origin and center. It is certain that the denial of only one of the attributes of the Divinity leads to disorder in all spheres and leads human society into the trance of death.

If, as I have said, these remarks to not appear entirely trivial to Your Eminence, then I would venture to ask you to place them at the feet of His Holiness, along with the homage rendered due to a most profound veneration and most high respect which I profess as a Catholic to his sacred person, his infallible judgments, and his inexorable rulings.

May God protect Your Eminence for many years. Kissing Your Eminence's hand is your attentive and sure servant.

—The Marquis of Valdegamas
Paris, 19 June 1852

NOTES

1. Raffaello Cardinal Fornari was the papal nuncio to France (1843–1850). He was a strong supporter of the Ultramontanists and closely tied to Louis Veuillot and the *L'Univers*. He was key advisor to Pius IX in the preparation of the *Syllabus of Errors*. This letter was written in response to a request from Cardinal Fornari seeking Donoso's analysis of the situation of the Church and of society at the time. The same request was sent to a number of other influential Ultramontanist figures, both ecclesiastical and lay. Among them were Louis-Edouard Cardinal Pie (Bishop of Poitiers), Cardinal Geissel (Archbishop of Cologne), Dom Prosper Gueranger (abbott of the Benedictine Abbey of Solesmes and influential liturgist), Louis Veuillot, and Emiliano Avogrado della Rotta (author of *Saggio intorno al socialismo e alle dottrine e tendenze socialistiche*). See Yves Chiron, *Pie IX: pape moderne* (Condé-sur-Noireau: Clovis, 1995).

2. Emile Girardin (1806–1881), celebrated French writer. The work in question is titled *L'abolition de l'autorité par la simplification du gouvernement* (1851).

Selected Bibliography

ORIGINAL WORKS

Donoso Cortés, Juan. *Antologia de Juan Donoso Cortés*. Ed. Francisco Elías de Tejada. Madrid: Editorial Tradicionalista, 1953.

———. *Artículos políticos en "El Porvenir."* Ed. Federico Súarez Verdeguer. Pamplona: Ediciones Universidad de Navarra, 1992.

———. *Donoso Cortés y la fundación de "El Heraldo" y "El Sol."* Ed. Federico Súarez Verdeguer. Pamplona: Ediciones Universidad de Navarra, 1986.

———. *Essai sur le catholicisme, le libéralisme et le socialisme*. Introduction by Arnaud Imatz. Bouère: Editions Dominique Martin Morin, 1986. French translation of the *Ensayo sobre el catolicismo, el liberalismo y el socialismo*.

———. *Essay on Catholicism, Liberalism, and Order*. Trans. Madeleine Vincent Goddard, ed. J. C. Reville. New York: Joseph F. Wagner, 1925. English translation of the *Ensayo*.

———. *Essays on Catholicism, Liberalism, and Socialism*. Trans. Rev. William McDonald. Dublin: M. H. Gill and Son, 1879. English translation of the *Ensayo*.

———. *Obras completas de Don Juan Donoso Cortés*, 2 vols. Ed. Juan Juretschke. Madrid: Biblioteca de Autores Cristianos, 1946.

———. *Obras completas de Donoso Cortés*, 2 vols. Ed. Carlos Valverde. Madrid: Biblioteca de Autores Cristianos, 1970.

———. *Der Staat Gottes*. Trans. Ludwig Fischer. Darmstadt: Wissenschaftliche Buchgesellschaft, 1966. German translation of the *Ensayo*.

———. "Speech on Dictatorship." In *Catholic Political Thought: 1789–1848*. Ed. Bela Menczer. South Bend: University of Notre Dame Press, 1962.

WORKS ON JUAN DONOSO CORTÉS

Armas, Gabriel de. *Donoso Cortés: su sentido trascendente de la vida.* Madrid: Colección Cálamo, 1953.

Brownson, Orestes. *Orestes Brownson: Selected Essays.* Ed. Russell Kirk. Chicago: Regnery, 1955.

Catholic Encyclopedia, 1909 edition. S.v. "Donoso Cortés," by Condé B. Pallen.

Chaix-Ruy, Jules. *Donoso Cortés: Théologien de l'histoire et prophète.* Paris: Beauchesne, 1956.

Copeland, Raymond F. *Donoso Cortés and His Social Thought.* Ph.D. dissertation. St. Louis: St. Louis University, 1950.

Dempf, Alois. *Christliche Staatsphilosophie in Spanien.* Salzburg: Verlag Anton Pustet, 1937.

Graham, John T. *Donoso Cortés: Utopian Romanticist and Political Realist.* Columbia: University of Missouri Press, 1974.

———. *Donoso Cortés on Liberalism.* Ph.D. dissertation. St. Louis: St. Louis University, 1957.

Heer, Friedrich. *Europe: Mother of Revolutions.* Trans. Charles Kessler and Jennetta Adcock. London: Weidenfield and Nicolson, 1971.

Herrera, R. A. *Donoso Cortés: Cassandra of the Age.* Grand Rapids: Eerdmans, 1995.

Hübner Gallo, Jorge Ivan. *Los católicos en la política.* Santiago: Zig-Zag, 1959.

Johnson, Jeffrey P. *Dogma and Dictatorship: The Political Thought of Juan Donoso Cortés.* Ph.D. dissertation. Ann Arbor: University Microfilms, 1999.

Kennedy, John J. *Donoso Cortés as a Servant of the State.* Ph.D. dissertation. New York: Columbia University, 1954.

Kuehnelt-Leddihn, Erik von. "Introduction." In Alexis de Toqueville, *Democracy in America,* vol. 1. Trans. Henry Reeve. New Rochelle: Arlington House, n.d.

———. *Leftism: From de Sade and Marx to Hitler and Marcuse.* New Rochelle: Arlington House, 1974.

Lease, Gary. *"Odd Fellows" in the Politics of Religion: Modernism, National Socialism, and German Judaism.* New York: Mouton de Gruyter, 1995.

Manion, Christopher. *The Philosophy of History of Juan Donoso Cortés.* Ph.D. dissertation. South Bend: University of Notre Dame, 1985.

Menéndez Pidal, Ramon. *La historia de España: la era Isabelina y el sexenio democrático (1834–1874),* vol. XXXIV. Madrid: Espasa Calpe, 1981.

Molnar, Thomas. *The Counter-Revolution.* New York: Funk & Wagnalls, 1969.

Neill, Thomas P. *They Lived the Faith.* Milwaukee: Bruce, 1951.

Papadakos, Catherine. *The Evolution of Donoso's Theory of Power.* Ph.D. dissertation. Ann Arbor: University Microfilms, 1980.

Pradera, Victor. *The New State.* Trans. Bernard Malley. London: Sands, 1939.

Saiz Barbera, Juan. *Pensamiento historico cristiano: ¿Vencerá el comunismo a Occidente?* Madrid: Ediciones Asociación Española de Lulianos, 1968.

Sánchez Abelenda, Raúl. *La teoría del poder en el pensamiento político de Juan Donoso Cortés.* Buenos Aires: Editorial Universitaria de Buenos Aires, 1969.

Schmitt, Carl. *La interpretación europea de Donoso Cortés.* Madrid: Rialp, 1953.

———. *Political Theology.* Trans. George Schwab. Cambridge: MIT Press, 1985.

Schramm, Edmund. *Donoso Cortés: ejemplo del pensamiento de la tradición.* Madrid: Publicaciones Españolas, 1961.

———. *Donoso Cortés: Su vida y su pensamiento.* Madrid: Espasa Calpe, 1936.

Schuettinger, Robert L., editor. *The Conservative Tradition in European Thought.* New York: Capricorn Books, 1970.

Súarez Verdeger, Federico. *Introducción a Donoso Cortés.* Madrid: Rialp, 1964.

Valverde, Carlos. "Introducción." In *Obras completas de Donoso Cortés*, vol. 1. Ed. Carlos Valverde. Madrid: Biblioteca de Autores Cristianos, 1970.

Viereck, Peter. *Conservatism: From John Adams to Churchill.* Princeton: D. Van Nostrand, 1956.

———. *Conservatism Revisited.* New York: Scribners, 1950.

Westemeyer, Dietmar. *Donoso Cortés, hombre de estado y teólogo.* Trans. J. S. Mazpule. Madrid: Editora Nacional, 1957.

Wilhelmsen, Frederick D. *Christianity and Political Philosophy.* Athens: University of Georgia Press, 1978.

Wilson, Francis G. *Political Thought in National Spain.* Champaign: Stipes, 1967.

Worden, Mark. *Juan Donoso Cortés.* Ph.D. dissertation. Chicago: University of Chicago, 1966.

ARTICLES ON JUAN DONOSO CORTÉS

Araquistáin, Luis de. "Donoso Cortés y su resonancia en Europa." *Cuadernos*, 3 (September–December 1953).

Armas, Gabriel de. "Donoso Cortés, maximo apologista y el *Syllabus*." *El Español* (7 December 1946).

Brophy, Leo. "Donoso Cortés: Statesman and Apologist." *Irish Monthly*, 78 (September 1950).

Brownson, Orestes. "Church and State." *Catholic World*, 5 (April 1867).

———. "Rights and Duties." *Brownson's Review* (October 1852).

Calvo Serer, Rafael. "Europa en 1949: Comentario a dos discursos de Donoso Cortés." *Arbor* (March 1949).

Cossio, Alfred de. "Donoso Cortés." *Dublin Review*, 220 (Spring 1947).

Fernandez de la Mora, Gonzalo. "Schmitt y Donoso ante la dictadura." *Razon Española*, 17 (May–June 1986).

Galindo Herrero, Santiago. "Donoso Cortés en la última etapa de su vida." *Arbor*, 25 (May 1953).

Herrera, Robert A. "Donoso Cortés: A Second Look at Political Apocalyptic." *Continuity*, 11 (1987).

———. "The Great in the Small: Donoso Cortés' Variation on a Theme from the *Civitas Dei*." *Augustiniana*, fascicles 1-4, 1988.

Kennedy, John J. "Donoso Cortés as a Servant of the State." *Review of Politics*, 14 (October 1952).

Lease, Gary. "Vatican Foreign Policy and the Origins of Modernism." Paper presented at the Seminar on Roman Catholic Modernism at the annual meeting of the American Academy of Religion, New Orleans, Louisiana, November 1996.

Letruria, P. "Previsión y refutación del ateísmo comunista en los últimos escritos de Juan Donoso Cortés." *Gregorianum*, 18 (1937).

Mayer, J. P. "Donoso Cortés' *De civitate Dei*." *Dublin Review*, 225: 451 (Spring 1951).

McMahon, H. G. "Story of the Conversion of Donoso Cortés." *Commonweal*, 509–535, 14 (1931).

Menczer, Bela. "A Prophet of Europe's Disasters." *The Month*, 183 (May 1947).

———. "Metternich and Donoso Cortés: Christian and Conservative Thought in the European Revolution." *Dublin Review*, 201 (last quarter 1948).

Neill, Thomas P. "Juan Donoso Cortés: Prophet of Our Time." *Catholic World*, 170 (November 1949).

———. "Juan Donoso Cortés: History and Prophecy." *Catholic Historical Review*, 40 (January 1955).

Ortiz Estrada, Luis. "Donoso Cortés, Veuillot y el *Syllabus* de Pio IX." *Reconquista*, 1 (1950).

Schmitt, Carl. "Der unbekannte Donoso Cortés." *Hochland*, Band 27, Heft 12 (September 1929).

RELATED WORKS

Aquinas, Thomas. *Compendium theologiæ*. Trans. Ross J. Dunn. Toronto: Saint Michael's College, 1934.

———. *In decem libros Ethicorum Aristotelis ad Nicomachum expositio*. Turin: Marietti, 1934.

———. *In librum beati Dionysii "De divinis nominibus" expositio*. Turin: Marietti, 1950.

———. *De regimine principum*. Turin: Marietti, 1924.

———. *Summa contra gentiles*. Trans. Anton Pegis. Garden City: Image, 1955.

———. *Summa theologiæ*. Trans. the fathers of the English Dominican Province. Chicago: Encyclopedia Britannica, 1952.

Arendt, Hannah. *The Origins of Totalitarianism*. New York: Harcourt Brace, 1973.

Artz, Frederick B. *The Mind of the Middle Ages*. Chicago: University of Chicago Press, 1980.

Augustine, St. Aurelius. *City of God*. Trans. Gerald G. Walsh, S. J., Demetrius B. Zema, S. J., Grace Monahan, O. S. U., and Daniel J. Honan. Ed. Vernon J. Bourke. Garden City: Image, 1958.

———. *Confessions*. Trans. Henry Chadwick. New York: Oxford University Press, 1991.

———. *The Enchiridion on Faith, Hope, and Love*. Trans. J. F. Shaw. Chicago: Regnery, 1961.

———. *De moribus ecclesiæ catholicæ*. Palermo: Edizioni Augustinus, 1991.

———. *The Political Writings*. Ed. Henry Paolucci. Chicago: Regnery, 1962.

Azpiazu, Joaquin. *The Corporate State*. St. Louis: Herder, 1951.

Balmes, Jaime. *Obras completas*, vol. 6. Ed. P. Casanovas, S. J. Madrid: Biblioteca de Autores Cristianos, 1950.

Barbu, Zevedei. *Democracy and Dictatorship: Their Psychology and Patterns of Life*. New York: Grove Press, 1956.

Bellah, Robert et alia, editors. *Habits of the Heart*. Berkeley: University of California Press, 1985.

Belloc, Hilaire. *The Crisis of Civilization*. New York: Fordham University Press, 1937.

———. *The Restoration of Property*. New York: Sheed and Ward, 1936.

———. *The Servile State.* Indianapolis: Liberty Classics, 1980.

Bendersky, Joseph W. *Carl Schmitt: Theorist for the Reich.* Princeton: Princeton University Press, 1983.

Bénichou, Paul. *Le temps des prophètes: Doctrines de l'âge romantique.* Paris: Gallimard, 1977.

Berdyaev, Nicolai. *The Meaning of the Creative Act.* Trans. Donald A. Lowrie. New York: Collier, 1962.

———. *The Meaning of History.* Trans. George Reavey. London: Geoffrey Bles, 1936.

———. *The Origin of Russian Communism.* Trans. R. M. French. London: Geoffrey Bles, 1955.

———. *Slavery and Freedom.* Trans. R. M. French. New York: Charles Scribner's Sons, 1944.

———. *Solitude and Society.* Trans. George Reavey. New York: Scribners, 1938.

Berlin, Isaiah. *The Crooked Timber of Humanity.* New York: Vintage, 1990.

———. *The Sense of Reality.* Ed. Henry Hardy. New York: Farrar, Straus and Giroux, 1996.

Blinkhorn, Martin, editor. *Fascists and Conservatives.* London: Unwin Hyman, 1990.

Bokenkotter, Thomas. *Church and Revolution: Catholics in the Struggle for Democracy and Social Justice.* New York: Doubleday, 1998.

———. *A Concise History of the Catholic Church.* Garden City: Doubleday, Image, 1979.

———. *Essential Catholicism: Dynamics of Faith and Belief.* New York: Doubleday, Image, 1986.

Bonald, Louis de. *Démonstration philosophique du principe constitutif de la société.* Paris: Vrin, 1985.

———. *Théorie du pouvoir politique et religieux.* Paris: Union Génerale d'Editions, 1966.

Buchanan, Tom and Conway, Martin, editors. *Political Catholicism in Europe, 1918–1965.* Oxford: Clarendon, 1996.

Burke, Edmund. *Reflections on the Revolution in France.* Ed. Conor Cruise O'Brien. Middlesex: Penguin Classics, 1986.

Calman, Alvin R. *Ledru-Rollin and the Second French Republic.* New York: Octagon Books, 1980.

Calvin, John. *Calvin's Institutes.* Ed. Hugh T. Kerr. Louisville: Westminster/John Knox Press, 1989.

Camus, Albert. *The Myth of Sisyphus and Other Essays.* Trans. Justin O'Brien. New York: Vintage, 1955.

———. *Notebooks: 1942-1951.* Trans. Justin O'Brien. New York: Paragon House, 1991.

———. *The Rebel.* Trans. Anthony Bower. New York: Vintage, 1956.

Carr, Raymond. *Spain: 1808–1975.* Oxford: Clarendon, 1982.

Carroll, David. *French Literary Fascism: Nationalism, Anti-Semitism, and the Ideology of Culture.* Princeton: Princeton University Press, 1995.

Carsten, F. L. *The Rise of Fascism.* London: Methuen, 1967.

Chesterton, G. K. *The Outline of Sanity.* New York: Dodd, Mead, and Company, 1927.

———. *Utopia of Usurers.* New York: Boni and Liveright, 1917.

Chiron, Yves. *Pie IX: pape moderne.* Condé-sur-Noireau: Clovis, 1995.

Clarke, H. Butler. *Modern Spain: 1815–1898.* New York: AMS Press, 1969.

Coppa, Frank J. *Pope Pius IX: Crusader in a Secular Age.* Boston: Twayne, 1979.

Corrêa de Oliveira, Plinio. *Révolution et contre-révolution.* São Paulo: Edições Catolicismo, 1960.

Corrin, Jay P. *G. K. Chesterton and Hilaire Belloc: The Battle Against Modernity.* Athens: Ohio University Press, 1981.

Cristi, Renato. *Carl Schmitt and Authoritarian Liberalism: Strong State, Free Economy.* Cardiff: University of Wales Press, 1998.

Daly, Mary. *Beyond God the Father: Toward a Philosophy of Women's Liberation.* Boston: Beacon Press, 1973.

Díez del Corral, Luis. *El liberalismo doctrinario.* Madrid: Instituto de Estudios Políticos, 1973.

Dostoyevsky, Fyodor. *The Brothers Karamazov.* Trans. Andrew H. MacAndrew. New York: Bantam, 1970.

Dupré, Louis. *Passage to Modernity.* New Haven: Yale University Press, 1993.

Dyzenhaus, David, editor. *Law as Politics: Carl Schmitt's Critique of Liberalism.* Durham: Duke University Press, 1998.

Elias de Tejado y Spinola, Francisco, Rafael Gambra Ciudad, and Francisco Puy Muñoz, editors. *¿Que es el carlismo?* Madrid: Escelicer, 1971.

Eliot, T. S. *The Idea of a Christian Society.* New York: Harcourt, Brace and Company, 1940.

———. *Notes Toward a Definition of Culture.* London: Faber and Faber, 1948.

Fijalkowski, Jürgen. *Die Wendung zum Führerstaat: Ideologische Komponenten in der politischen Philosophie Carl Schmitts.* Cologne: Westdeutscher Verlag, 1958.

Flannery, Austin, editor. *Vatican Council II: The Conciliar and Post Conciliar Documents.* Boston: St. Paul Editions, 1975.

Fraga Iribarne, Manuel. *El pensamiento conservador español.* Barcelona: Editora Planeta, 1981.

Freire, Paulo. *Education for Critical Consciousness.* Trans. Myra Bergman Ramos. New York: Continuum, 1994.

———. *Pedagogy of the Oppressed.* Trans. Myra Bergman Ramos. New York: Continuum, 1994.

Freud, Sigmund. *Civilization and Its Discontents.* Trans. James Strachey. New York: Norton, 1961.

———. *The Future of an Illusion.* Trans. W. D. Robson-Scott. Garden City: Doubleday, 1961.

Fritzsche, Klaus. *Politische Romantik und Gegenrevolution: Fluchtwege in der Krise der bürgerlichen Gesellschaft–Das Beispiel des "Tat" Kreises.* Frankfurt: Suhrkamp, 1976.

Fromm, Erich. *Escape from Freedom.* New York: Avon, 1965.

———. *Man for Himself.* New York: Henry Holt, 1947.

———. *The Sane Society.* New York: Henry Holt, 1955.

Fukuyama, Francis. *The End of History and the Last Man.* New York: Avon, 1992.

García-Llera, José Luis Comellas, editor. *Historia general de España y America*, vol. XIV. Madrid: Rialp, 1983.

Germino, Dante. *Machiavelli to Marx: Modern Western Political Thought.* Chicago: University of Chicago Press, 1972.

Gilson, Étienne. *A Gilson Reader.* Ed. Anton Pegis. Garden City: Image, 1957.

———. *God and Philosophy.* New Haven: Yale University Press, 1941.

Girard, René. *A Girard Reader.* Ed. James G. Williams. New York: Crossroad, 1996.

———. *Violence and the Sacred.* Trans. Patrick Gregory. Baltimore: John Hopkins University Press, 1977.

Godechot, Jacques. *La contre-révolution.* Paris: Presses Universitaires de France, 1961.

Gottfried, Paul Edward. *Carl Schmitt: Politics and Theory.* New York: Greenwood, 1990.

Gough, Austin. *Paris and Rome: The Gallican Church and the Ultramontane Campaign, 1848-1853.* Oxford: Clarendon Press, 1986.

Griffin, Roger. *The Nature of Fascism.* New York: Routledge, 1993.

Griffin, Roger, editor. *International Fascism: Theories, Causes and the New Consensus.* London: Oxford University Press, 1998.

———. *Fascism.* New York: Oxford University Press, 1995.

Gutiérrez, Gustavo. *A Theology of Liberation.* Trans. and ed. Sister Caridad Inda and John Eagleson. New York: Orbis, 1973.

Habermas, Jürgen. *A Berlin Republic: Writings on Germany.* Trans. Steven Rendell. Lincoln: University of Nebraska Press, 1997.

———. *The New Conservatism: Cultural Criticism and the Historians Debate.* Edited and Trans. Shierry Weber Nicholsen. Cambridge: MIT Press, 1989.

Havel, Václav. *The Art of the Impossible: Politics as Morality in Practice.* Trans. Paul Wilson and others. New York: Alfred A. Knopf, 1997.

———. *Letters to Olga.* Trans. Paul Wilson. New York: Henry Holt, 1989.

———. *Living in Truth.* Ed. Jan Vladislav. Boston: Faber and Faber, 1986.

———. *Open Letters.* Trans. and ed. Paul Wilson. New York: Knopf, 1991.

Hegel, G. W. F. *Introduction to the Philosophy of History.* Trans. Leo Rauch. Indianapolis: Hackett, 1988.

Herf, Jeffrey. *Reactionary Modernism: Technology, Culture, and Politics in Weimar and the Third Reich.* New York: Cambridge University Press, 1984.

Heyer, Friedrich. *The Catholic Church: From 1846 to 1870.* Trans. D. W. D. Shaw. London: Adam and Charles Black, 1969.

Hirschman, Albert O. *The Rhetoric of Reaction: Perversity, Futility, Jeopardy.* Cambridge: Belknap Press, 1991.

Hobbes, Thomas. *Leviathan.* Ed. Edwin Curley. Indianapolis: Hackett, 1994.

Hoffer, Eric. *The True Believer.* New York: HarperCollins, 1951.

Holmes, Stephen. *The Anatomy of Antiliberalism.* Cambridge: Harvard University Press, 1993.

Holt, Edgar. *The Carlist Wars in Spain.* Chester Springs: Dufour Editions, 1967.

Hunhold, Albert, editor. *Freedom and Serfdom.* Dordrecht: D. Reidel, 1961.

Ihm, Claudia Carlen, editor. *The Papal Encyclicals: 1740–1878.* Wilmington: McGrath, 1981. Contains the encyclical letters of Pius IX.

Johnson, Paul. *A History of Christianity.* New York: Atheneum, 1976.

Kaes, Anton, Martin Jay, and Edward Dimendberg, editors. *The Weimar Republic Sourcebook.* Berkeley: University of California Press, 1994.

Kiernan, V. G. *The Revolution of 1854 in Spanish History.* Oxford: Clarendon, 1966.

Kirk, Russell. *The Conservative Mind: From Burke to Eliot.* Chicago: Regnery, 1960.

Küng, Hans. *On Being a Christian.* Trans. Edward Quinn. Garden City: Doubleday, Image, 1976.

———. *Infallibility?: An Inquiry.* Trans. Edward Quinn. Garden City: Doubleday, 1971.

———. *Theology for the Third Millenium.* Trans. Peter Heinegg. New York: Doubleday, Anchor, 1988.

Laqueur, Walter, editor. *Fascism: A Readers Guide.* Berkeley: University of California Press, 1976.

Leo XIII. *The Church Speaks to the Modern World: The Social Teachings of Leo XIII.* Ed. Étienne Gilson. Garden City: Doubleday, Image, 1954. The collected social encyclicals of Leo XIII.

Locke, John. *A Letter Concerning Toleration.* Buffalo: Prometheus Books, 1990.

———. *Second Treatise of Government.* Ed. C.B. McPherson. Indianapolis: Hackett, 1980.

Lonergan, Bernard J. F., S. J. *Collection.* Ed. Frederick E. Crowe, S. J. Montreal: Palm, 1967.

———. *A Third Collection: Papers by Bernard J. F. Lonergan.* Ed. Frederick E. Crowe. New York: Paulist Press, 1985.

Machiavelli, Niccolò. *The Discourses.* Trans. Leslie Walker, S. J. New York: Penguin, 1970.

———. *The Prince.* Trans. Harvey C. Mansfield, Jr. Chicago: University of Chicago Press, 1985.

Maeztu, Ramiro de. *Ensayos.* Buenos Aires: Emecé Editores, 1948.

———. *El nuevo tradicionalismo y la revolución social.* Madrid: Editora Nacional, 1959.

Maistre, Joseph de. *Considerations on France.* Trans. Richard A. Lebrun. Montreal: McGill-Queen's University Press, 1974.

———. *Œuvres complètes*, vol. 5. Geneva: Slatkine, 1979.

———. *Du Pape dans son rapport avec les souverainetés temporelles.* Paris: Librairie Catholique Emmanuel Vitte, 1928.

———. *The Works of Joseph de Maistre.* Edited and Trans. Jack Lively. New York: Schocken, 1971.

Marcel, Gabriel. *Homo viator.* Trans. Emma Crauford. New York: Harper and Row, 1962.

———. *Man Against Mass Society.* Trans. G. S. Fraser. New York: University Press of America, 1985.

———. *The Mystery of Being*, vol. 1. Trans. G. S. Fraser. New York: University Press of America, 1978.

———. *The Mystery of Being*, vol. 2. Trans. René Hague. New York: University Press of America, 1979.

Marcuse, Herbert. *One-Dimensional Man.* Boston: Beacon Press, 1964.

Martinell Gifre, Francisco. *La política con alas: José Antonio, Ramiro y Onésimo desde una perspectiva actual.* Madrid: Ediciones del Movimiento, 1974.

Marty, Albert. *L'Action française: racontée par elle-même.* Paris: Nouvelles Éditions Latines, 1968.

Marx, Karl and Friedrich Engels. *The Communist Manifesto.* Trans. Samuel Moore. London: Penguin, 1967.

Massis, Henri. *Defence of the West.* Trans. F. S. Flint. New York: Harcourt, Brace, and Company, 1928.

Maurras, Charles. *Mes idées politiques.* Paris: Fayard, 1937.

McCormick, John P. *Carl Schmitt's Critique of Liberalism: Against Politics as Technology.* Cambridge: University of Cambridge Press, 1997.

Meier, Heinrich. *Carl Schmitt and Leo Strauss: The Hidden Dialogue.* Trans. J. Harvey Lomax. Chicago: University of Chicago Press, 1995.

———. *Die Lehre Carl Schmitts: Vier Kapitel zur Unterscheidung Politischer Theologie und Politischer Philosophie.* Stuttgart: Verlag J. B. Metzler, 1994.

Michnik, Adam. *Letters from Freedom: Post-Cold War Realities and Perspectives.* Ed. Irena Grudzinska Gross, trans. Jane Cave. Berkeley: University of California Press, 1998.

Milfull, John, editor. *The Attractions of Fascism.* New York: Berg, 1990.

Mill, John Stuart. *On Liberty.* Ed. Elizabeth Rapaport. Indianapolis: Hackett, 1978.

Milosz, Czeslaw. *The Captive Mind.* Trans. Jane Zielonko. New York: Vintage, 1953.

Mohler, Armin. *Die Konservative Revolution in Deutschland: 1918–1932.* Darmstadt: Wissenschaftliche Buchgesellschaft, 1972.

Momigliano, Arnaldo. *On Pagans, Jews, and Christians.* Middletown: Wesleyan University Press, 1987.

Monsegú, Bernardo. *Religión y política: el cristianismo y la orden religiosa de la sociedad.* Madrid: Editorial Coculsa, 1974.

Mourret, Fernand. *A History of the Catholic Church*, vol. 8. Trans. Newton Thompson. St. Louis: Herder, 1957.

Mühlberger, Detlef, editor. *The Social Basis of European Fascist Movements.* London: Croom Helm, 1987.

Murray, John Courtney, S. J. *We Hold These Truths.* New York: Sheed and Ward, 1960.

Neocleous, Mark. *Fascism.* Minneapolis: University of Minnesota Press, 1997.

Neuner, J., S. J. and J. Dupuis, S. J., editors. *The Christian Faith in the Doctrinal Documents of the Catholic Church.* New York: Alba, 1982.

Nietzsche, Friedrich. *Beyond Good and Evil.* Trans. Walter Kaufmann. New York: Vintage, 1966.

———. *On the Genealogy of Morals.* Trans. Walter Kaufmann. New York: Vintage, 1967.

Noack, Paul. *Carl Schmitt: Eine Biographie.* Frankfurt/Main: Propyläen, 1993.

Nolte, Ernst. *Three Faces of Fascism: Action Française, Italian Fascism, National Socialism.* New York: Holt Rhinehart & Winston, 1969.

Novak, Michael. *Freedom with Justice: Catholic Social Thought and Liberal Institutions.* San Francisco: Harper and Row, 1984.

Ortega y Gasset, José. *Man and Crisis.* Trans. Mildred Adams. New York: W. W. Norton, 1958.

———. *The Revolt of the Masses.* New York: W. W. Norton, 1932.

Palacio Atard, Vicente. *La España del siglo XIX: 1808–1898.* Madrid: Espasa Calpe, 1981.

Palaver, Wolfgang. *Die mythischen Quellen des Politischen: Carl Schmitts Freund-Feind-Theorie.* Stuttgart: Kohlhammer, 1998.

Payne, Stanley. *Fascism: Comparison and Definition.* Madison: University of Wisconsin Press, 1980.

———. *A History of Fascism: 1914–1945.* Madison: University of Wisconsin Press, 1995.

Pétain, Philippe. *Actes et ecrits.* Ed. Jacques Isorni. Paris: Flammarion, 1974.

Peterson, Erik. *Der Monotheismus als politisches Problem.* Leipzig: Jakob Hegner, 1935.

Pike, F. and T. Stritch., editors. *The New Corporatism.* South Bend: University of Notre Dame Press, 1974.

Pilch, Martin. *System des transcendentalen Etatismus: Staat und Verfassung bei Carl Schmitt.* Vienna: Karolinger, 1994.

Pius XI. *The Church and the Reconstruction of the Modern World: The Social Encyclicals of Pius XI.* ed. Terence B. McLaughlin. Garden City: Image, 1957.

Plato. *The Dialogues of Plato.* Trans. B. Jowett. New York: Random House, 1937.

Ploncard d'Assac, Jacques. *Salazar*, 2nd ed. Bouère: Dominique Martin Morin, 1983.

Preston, Paul. *Franco.* San Francisco: HarperCollins, 1994.

Primo de Rivera, José Antonio. *Obras de José Antonio Primo de Rivera*, 8th edition. Ed. Agustín del Rio Cisneros. Madrid: Delegación de la Sección Femenina del Movimiento, 1974.

Proudhon, Pierre-Joseph. *Œuvres complètes*, vol. 1. Ed. C. Bouglé and H. Moysset. Paris: Slatkine, 1982.

Quaritsch, Helmut. *Positionen und Begriffe Carl Schmitts.* Berlin: Duncker & Humblot, 1989.

Roo, Willian A. van, S. J. *Grace and Original Justice According to St. Thomas.* Rome: Pontifical Gregorian University Press, 1955.

Rousseau, Jean-Jacques. *The Basic Political Writings.* Trans. and ed. Donald A. Cress. Indianapolis: Hackett, 1987.

———. *Émile.* Trans. Barbara Foxley. Rutland: Charles E. Tuttle, 1995.

Salazar, António de Oliveira. *Salazar (Prime Minister of Portugal) Says . . . .* Lisbon: SPN Books, n.d.

Schama, Simon. *Citizens: A Chronicle of the French Revolution.* New York: Vintage, 1989.

Schmitt, Carl. *The Concept of the Political.* Trans. George Schwab. Chicago: University of Chicago Press, 1996.

———. *The Crisis of Parliamentary Democracy.* Trans. Ellen Kennedy. Cambridge: MIT Press, 1988.

———. *Die Diktatur: Von den Anfängen des modernen Souveränitätsgedankens bis zum proletarischen Klassenkampf.* Berlin: Duncker & Humblot, 1989.

———. *La dictadura.* Trans. José Díaz García. Madrid: Alianza, 1985. Spanish translation of *Die Diktatur.*

———. *Political Romanticism.* Trans. Guy Oakes. Cambridge: MIT Press, 1986.

———. *Roman Catholicism and Political Form.* Trans. G. L. Ulmen. Westport: Greenwood Press, 1996.

Schüddekopf, Otto-Ernst. *Linke Leute von Rechts: Nationalbolschewismus in Deutschland 1918–1933.* Frankfurt: Ullstein, 1972.

Schwab, George. *The Challenge of the Exception: An Introduction to the Political Ideas of Carl Schmitt between 1921 and 1936*, 2nd ed. Westport: Greenwood, 1989.

Scruton, Roger. *The Meaning of Conservatism.* London: Macmillan, 1980.

Simon, Yves. *A General Theory of Authority.* Notre Dame: University of Notre Dame Press, 1980.

Somerville, John and Ronald E. Santoni, editors. *Social and Political Philosophy.* New York: Doubleday, 1963.

Sontheimer, Kurt. *Antidemokratisches Denken in Deutschland: 1918–1932.* Munich: Nymphenburger Verlagshandlung, 1968.

Sorel, Georges. *Reflections on Violence.* Trans. T. E. Hulme. London: George Allen & Unwin, 1915.

Soros, George. *The Crisis of Global Capitalism: Open Society Endangered.* New York: Public Affairs, 1998.

Soucy, Robert. *French Fascism: The Second Wave, 1933–1939.* New Haven: Yale University Press, 1995.

The Spanish Constitution: The Fundamental Laws of the State. Madrid: Imprenta del Ministerio de Informaciön y Turismo, 1972.

Spengler, Oswald. *The Decline of the West*, 2 vols. Ed. and trans. Charles Francis Atkinson. New York : A. A. Knopf, 1939.

Stern, Fritz Richard. *The Politics of Cultural Despair: A Study in the Rise of Germanic Ideology.* Garden City: Anchor, 1965.

Sternhell, Zeev. *Neither Right nor Left: Fascist Ideology in France.* Princeton: Princeton University Press, 1986.

Strauss, Leo. *Natural Right and History.* Chicago: University of Chicago Press, 1953.

———. *Thoughts on Machiavelli.* Chicago: University of Chicago Press, 1984.

Taubes, Jacob, editor. *Der Fürst dieser Welt: Carl Schmitt und die Folgen.* Munich: Wilhelm Fink Verlag/Verlag Ferdinand Schöningh, 1983.

Taylor, Charles. *The Ethics of Authenticity.* Cambridge: Harvard University Press, 1991.

Thomas, Hugh. *The Spanish Civil War.* New York: Harper and Row, 1963.

Tierney, Brian, editor. *The Middle Ages: Sources of Medieval History*, vol. 1. New York: Alfred A. Knopf, 1978.

Tinder, Glenn. *The Political Meaning of Christianity.* San Francisco: HarperCollins, 1989.

Tocqueville, Alexis de. *Democracy in America.* Trans. Henry Reeve. New Rochelle: Arlington House, n.d.

Veuillot, Louis. *L'Illusion libérale.* Paris: Dismas, 1986.

Voegelin, Eric. *Anamnesis: Zur Theorie der Geschichte und Politik.* Munich: Piper, 1966.

———. *Political Religions.* Trans. T. J. DiNapoli and E. S. Easterly, III. Lewiston: The Edwin Mellen Press, 1986.

———. *Science, Politics, and Gnosticism.* Trans. William J. Fitzpatrick. Chicago: Regnery, 1968.

Wacker, Bernd, editor. *Die eigentlich katholische Verschärfung: Konfession, Theologie und Politik im Werk Carl Schmitts.* Munich: Wilhelm Fink Verlag, 1994.

Widengren, Geo. *Mani and Manichæism.* Trans. Charles Kessler. New York: Holt, Rinehart and Winston, 1965.

Woolf, S. J., editor. *European Fascism.* New York: Vintage, 1969.

RELATED ARTICLES

Bendersky, Joseph. "Carl Schmitt and the Conservative Revolution." *Telos* 72 (Summer 1987).

Lilla, Mark. "The Enemy of Liberalism." *The New York Review of Books* (15 May 1997).

Novak, Michael. "Saving Distributism." *The Chesterton Review*, 10 (February 1984).

Rao, John C. "Louis Veuillot and Catholic "Intransigence:' A Re-evaluation." *Faith and Reason*, IX, 4 (Winter 1983).

Wilhelmsen, Alexandra. "The Carlist Motto, 'Dios, Patria, Fueros, Rey,' in the Late Nineteenth Century." *Society for Spanish and Portuguese Historical Studies Bulletin*, IV, 7 (September 1979).

———. "Carlos VII or an Introduction to Carlism." *Iberian Studies*, VIII, 1 (Spring 1979).

Wilhelmsen, Frederick D. "¿Hay una filosofia política católica?" *Verbo*, 307–308 (1992).

Index

About the Editor

JEFFREY P. JOHNSON is an independent researcher and translator. Dr. Johnson taught at Boston College for seven years as an adjunct faculty member. Currently he is preparing a new critical English edition of Donoso Cortés' *Essay on Catholicism, Liberalism, and Socialism.*

Recent Titles in
Contributions in Political Science

International Theory: To the Brink and Beyond
Andrew P. Dunne

To Sheathe the Sword: Civil-Military Relations in the Quest for Democracy
John P. Lovell and David E. Albright, editors

President Reagan and the World
Eric J. Schmertz, Natalie Datlof, and Alexej Ugrinsky, editors

Ronald Reagan's America
Eric J. Schmertz, Natalie Datlof, and Alexej Ugrinsky, editors

Germany for the Germans? The Political Effects of International Migration
Wesley D. Chapin

Out of Russian Orbit: Hungary Gravitates to the West
Andrew Felkay

Ideas of Social Order in the Ancient World
Vilho Harle

Voting Rights and Redistricting in the United States
Mark E. Rush, editor

Democratization in Late Twentieth-Century Africa: Coping with Uncertainty
Jean-Germain Gros, editor

Eisenhower's Executive Office
Alfred Dick Sander

Partisanship and the Birth of America's Second Party, 1796–1800: "Stop the Wheels of Government"
Matthew Q. Dawson

The Early Security Confederations: From the Ancient Greeks to the United Colonies of New England
Frederick K. Lister

ISBN 0-313-31397-0

HARDCOVER BAR CODE